"THE STRAD" LIBRARY, No. XXIII.

The Art of Violin Playing

FOR PLAYERS AND TEACHERS

BY

FRANK THISTLETON

AUTHOR OF
"Modern Violin Technique: How to acquire it; How to teach it."

London:
"THE STRAD" Office, 2, Duncan Terrace, London, N. 1.
HORACE MARSHALL & SON, 46, Farringdon Street, E.C. 4.
New York:
CHARLES SCRIBNER'S SONS, 597-599, Fifth Avenue.
1924.

Printed in Great Britain by
J. H. Lavender and Co.,
2, Duncan Terrace, City Road, London, N.

PREFACE.

THE READER will find one or two short passages in italics, and for these it is necessary to offer an apology. I have committed the unpardonable offence of quoting myself! This is with no intention to be original or because of such unbounded faith in my own statements, but merely that I lack the ability to express my thoughts more concisely. Therefore, I ask the reader's pardon.

For the rest, I can only say that that which I have written is the result of many years' quiet thought and observation in connection with my own teaching, and however inadequate the work may be, I am at least hopeful that it will have the effect of causing others to apply their abilities to a subject which has not been overstated by teachers.

Should players doubt any statements they can disprove or verify the broad principles by observing the performances of well-known violinists. I am fain to maintain that all fiddle-players use the same methods, but with slight variation to suit their own peculiar requirements.

The shortcomings and omissions are in all probability numerous. The former are unintentional, but in certain instances matter which was not considered relevant to the general plan of the work has been discarded. This will account for some of the omissions.

It has been my endeavour to keep to essentials without becoming involved in a maze of details wherein the main issues could easily be lost sight of. My experience has been that it is easy to observe peculiarities, but that essentials escape notice on account of the simple fact that they *are* essentials. They are so necessarily a part of the whole as to attract no attention.

My remarks are applicable to no particular "School" or "Method," they are merely intended to convey broad common-sense views, the utility of which players may test for themselves.

The reader will appreciate the difficulty in writing about such a subject. It is one thing to illustrate each point with the pupil before one and another to express one's thoughts on paper so as to apply equally to all players.

F. T.

CONTENTS.

PART I.

CHAPTER IV.

ADVICE TO BEGINNERS.

PART II.

CHAPTER V.

THE LEFT SIDE OF THE BODY.

CHAPTER VI.

THE RIGHT SIDE OF THE BODY (THE BOW ARM).

CHAPTER VII.

THE BOW ARM (*Continued*).

CHAPTER VIII.

THE BOW ARM (*Continued*).

CHAPTER IX.

THE BOW ARM (*Continued*).

CHAPTER X.

THE BOW ARM (*Continued*).

PART III.

CHAPTER XI.

CHAPTER XII.

CHAPTER XIII.

CHAPTER XIV.

SLIDING.

CHAPTER XV.

PART IV.

CHAPTER XVI.

BOWING.

CHAPTER XVII.

CHAPTER XVIII.

PART V.

CHAPTER XIX.

CHAPTER XX.

CHAPTER XXI.

CHAPTER XXII.

PART VI.

CHAPTER XXIII.

CHAPTER XXIV.

CHAPTER XXV.

CHAPTER XXVI.

CHAPTER XXVII.

LIST OF ILLUSTRATIONS.

PLATES.

DIAGRAMS.

> " By music minds an equal temper know,
> Nor swell too high, nor sink too low."
>
> *Pope.*

The Art of Violin Playing

FOR PLAYERS AND TEACHERS

PART I.

CHAPTER I.

1. EXPLANATION.

IN the present book it will be my endeavour to develop the principles of bow and finger technique already outlined in my "Modern Violin Technique." Therefore, I propose going through the whole of violin technique assuming that I am dealing with a pupil who knows nothing about the subject. Perhaps if the order of the work is explained in advance there will be less likelihood of a misunderstanding as to my intentions.

Following a chapter to give a sense of perspective, I shall make a few general remarks on Technique, then follow this by a short chapter on Tone, and after dealing with the method of holding the violin, Bow Technique, then Finger, or Left Hand Technique. Parts IV to VI will be devoted to the consideration of Advanced Technique.

Let me explain why the subjects are taken in this order.

(1) The meaning of technique must be clearly realised before any study can be undertaken.

(2) No attempt to produce tone should be made until the term is understood.

(3) Bow Technique must be mastered before Finger Technique is of any account.

That each should be understood without confusion with the other, I propose dealing with them separately, though in actual practice they are of necessity studied conjointly.

ARGUMENT.

2. ON ESSENTIALS.

Three essentials are necessary to ensure the success of the individual who decides to take up the study of an instrument.

Provided that there exists what, for want of a better name, we may call natural musical ability, he must be able :—

(1) To understand.
(2) To feel.
(3) To express.

No one of these attributes is *by itself* of any service in the development of any artist—each leads to the other—and it is their combination that makes art possible.

3. ON UNDERSTANDING.

First and foremost the artist must understand. I might better have said that he must have understanding. He should have knowledge, a fine imagination, a responsive temperament, self-control, self-criticism, a sense of proportion, of humour, a keen, well-tempered perception, and a thousand other assets that do not necessarily form part of the working machinery of individuals in other walks of life.

Understanding is necessary before expression is possible. Unless by instinct or subconsciously, we can only accomplish that which we understand. Before the most commonplace everyday tasks are undertaken, we have to realise that which we are about to do, how we intend it should be carried out and what the result should be. Now if we must be in possession of this knowledge when washing up the dishes we must at least know as much when practising the violin.

In order to be able to study with advantage we must understand:—

(1) That which is to be done.
(2) How it should be accomplished.
(3) What the result should be.

I merely mention this, as we all know how often we are shown the result without having anything but an indefinite idea how it has been arrived at.

4. ON FEELING.

Understanding is of no avail without feeling. By "feeling" I do not mean the exhibition of uncontrolled emotions or a heart that all the world can perceive is merely dangling from one's watch chain. Sincere feeling is a resultant of understanding. The power to feel the things that matter in life. The amazing magnificence of life, the joy of being, of quiet thought, of sweet content, of conviction, knowledge, sympathy, sincerity, faith, love, hope, joy, sorrow, unselfish devotion, purity, strength, youth, courage, honour, poverty, and, above all, that inner knowledge of the spiritual significance of all art.

When understanding and feeling are present there is in all probability something worth saying, but without knowledge of a medium of expression one remains as incoherent as the village pump—in fact infinitely more so and far less useful. Therefore, one requires a thorough knowledge and a facile application of one's medium which is described as technique.

5. ON EXPRESSION.

There are two kinds of artists:—

(1) Creative.

(2) Interpretative.

Under the first we get productive artists such as composers; in the second instance we have executants who present that which has been created.

We might sub-divide the interpretative artists as follows :—(1) Artists, (2) Virtuosi. Let me explain the difference between the two, and then leave you to judge which is the true artist.

(1) The interpretative artist is the medium of expression whereby the thoughts of great masters are made known to us. The one aim of an interpretative artist is to show you the work and genius of another man—as far as is possible in the light in which he would have presented it—without coming too much into the picture himself.

(2) The virtuoso is the medium for expressing himself. He shows you what he can do with his instrument, and astonishes you by the perfection of his technique, etc. Incidentally he may show you other things, but he is unable to keep himself altogether out of the limelight.

There are many fine shades and distinctions that can be drawn between the artist and virtuoso that I have not touched upon, and it is not altogether necessary that I should do so, but the above is, in the main, a rough description that will suffice for general purposes.

Without taking any definite examples, it is easy to perceive that various performances of the same work by different musicians differ in important respects. You find that by comparison you admire certain outstanding "qualities" in every well-known executive artist. You adore Mr. Voluptuousness's tone, Mr. Blacksmith's power, Mr. Lack-Control's abandon, Mr. Weak-Knee's delicacy, Mr. Cold's reserve, Mr. Heat's warmth and Mr. Make-Believe's "show-off." Yet do you stop to think whether a due sense of proportion has been retained or why such assets incite your admiration, and if they are employed in conjunction with other and equally necessary means of expression in order to realise the high aims of the composer? It may be Mr. Voluptousness's one aim to produce a beautiful, sensuous tone, Mr. Blacksmith's to glory in power and strength, Mr. Lack-Control's to wallow in the mire, Mr. Weak-Knee's ambition to tickle you with a feather, and Mr. Make-Believe's desire to pander to your stupidity.

Certain qualities are good only in proportion to other qualities; it is the *balance* that really matters.

Just think one moment. Should tone (or any one quality) be admired to the exclusion of all else? Are there other factors to be considered in the repertory of an artist?

At one time or another I suppose we have all been led away by the brilliance of some technical achievement. It is thin ice, however, that does not carry a great deal of weight. Even the finished technique is merely the beginning of things; a very necessary beginning, but still the beginning.

CHAPTER II.

6. ON TECHNIQUE.

PERHAPS no individuals (with the possible exception of golfers!) suffer such tortures, confusion and disappointments as violinists. The instrument is sufficiently difficult provided that a helping hand is extended at the cross-roads, but it is impossible to arrive anywhere without a signpost.

Almost every would-be violinist has suffered innumerable setbacks during his or her weary climb to the top rung of the ladder, merely because the steps were so imperfectly designed. There has been so much confusion of thought and execution, when all have been working towards the same goal, viz., a knowledge of certain *general* principles upon which violin technique is founded.

Many have spent their lives in a labyrinth of unimportant details which either they or their teachers described by the priceless misnomer of "school," while the broad theory applicable to all violin technique has been lost sight of.

Perhaps it is on account of the difficulty found in applying the same technique to different individuals that the chief misunderstandings have arisen. The principles of violin technique remain the same; individuals are different.

We must realise that no two pupils, taught by the same teacher on exactly the same lines, will ever play alike. The numerous fine violinists taught by those remarkable teachers Auer and Sevcik all obtain their results in slightly different ways, but the *essentials* are there, and, therefore, their playing is entirely satisfactory. It is necessary to concentrate on essentials, the side lines will appear as a result of your having a surplus from your main stock.

Every teacher and student aims at obtaining the best results with the least possible labour. The labour is all sufficient if the path is cleared of thorns, otherwise progress must be hampered. As the road is being travelled we should be in a position to see the horizon gradually opening out to our view, the wonderful horizon that is never quite reached.

Art cannot be conquered, technique may be.

7. WHAT IS TECHNIQUE?

Now let us try to decide what technique is. What is it . . . ? Is it the manner in which technique is employed that makes the highest art possible or is technique the art itself?

If we allow the second supposition, we find ourselves up against the fact that the technique of an art remains the *medium* of expression. The medium of expressing what . . . . . ? We are forced to the conclusion that there *must* be something to be attained higher than technical facility.

That which is of account in every art is the ultimate use to which technique is put —the manner in which the artist uses his working capital.

Let us take a simile—a language. We may learn all the words in a dictionary and still remain inexpressive. Without a knowledge of the meaning and the relative position of words, phrases, sentences, etc., it is not possible to converse. Yet again, we may have this knowledge and have nothing to say worth expressing! Therefore, the qualities that are most necessary in order that we may use our technique so as to achieve the finest results are the higher ones of the mind.

There must be understanding and feeling as previously described, before expression is possible, or rather—of any account.

Do not confuse mere technique with art. The art is in concealing technique, not displaying it.

In the performance of all serious music the technique is the means (the language, as it were) by which musical thought is expressed. "Technique is merely an acquired facility which must necessarily be attained in order that musical ideas may be expressed sanely and naturally. The study of technique is like the study of words which require inspiration or weighty thought to give them expression."

Now the object of all this preliminary preamble is in order to give the pupil a sense of perspective to enable him to realise that technique is a means to an end—not the end itself—and to emphasise the importance of keeping technique in its proper place. I want to convince my readers that technique is the very beginning of things—the elements, as it were, of any art. Therefore it is essential that we do not make a god of technique, for its own sake, but, at least, assure ourselves that it is our servant.

8. HOW TO OBTAIN TECHNIQUE.

Many art students begin by endeavouring to complete the traceries before laying the foundations, but we all know that it is necessary to build our house before we start decorating it.

Stick to the foundations until you are quite sure they are well and truly laid, then you will have something upon which to build. You cannot go quickly to begin with.

Violinists spend endless time and labour on side lines, frills, feathers and powder-puffs hardly calculated to assist them in serious study. At the outset they approach their labours in the wrong light. Valuable time is devoted by the enthusiast to the mastering, by hopeless methods, of technical difficulties (and difficulties that are not technical) which could be overcome so much more easily by taking a little thought.

It is important to realise that most of our troubles are mental—they certainly are not physical.

In order not to waste time on useless practice, *understand* every movement before you attempt its execution. We can only do that which we do not understand by instinct, or through a "fluke," and it is unlikely, in these circumstances, that we will be able to repeat the performance whenever we want to.

When we realise that which we are attempting, we can apply our knowledge and constantly employ the same method until it proves successful. This constant application of the same means to acquire the same end leads in the long run to our technique becoming "second nature." Consequently, after a time, it is not necessary to think *how* we do things, but it is essential that we know how we obtain certain results whilst we are practising.

Good technique simply means good machinery, and the better the technique the easier is it to give expression to that which one thinks and feels.

CHAPTER III.

TONE.

9. DEFINITION.

TONE is a definition applied to vibrations of a more or less pleasant character. The screech of a railway engine whistle is easily recognised as "noise," but the sound produced from a musical instrument (when played upon by a skilled performer) is described as "tone." Noise is the result of crude discordant vibrations. Tone is the harmony of regular musical sound waves.

Between tone and noise there are many differentiations. With noise we are not greatly concerned, but in tone there are variations as between the shrew and the schoolboy, the knave and the saint.

Amongst human beings we have various classes of individuals whose chief characteristics we can place under certain definite headings, such as weak, strong, cold, warm, round, hollow, harsh, loud, forced, natural, etc. Tone may be described as being weak, strong, cold, warm, round, hollow, harsh, loud, forced, natural, metallic, nasal or woody, etc. (the latter definitions would equally apply to some individuals!) The terms are in any case applicable to our friends, so that it is not difficult to understand them in relation to musical sounds.

Good tone is always sincere and natural, bad tone artificial.

Tone should not be confused with pitch; the former may remain excellent when the latter is anything but true, though one is of little effect without the other.

10. VOLUME AND QUALITY.

Strictly speaking, tone should not be applied to quantity, as it relates to the *quality* of musical sound. Tone is none the less beautiful because it is not big, and there is no satisfactory excuse for a loud tone becoming harsh. It is better that tone remains small and pleasant—otherwise tone has merely degenerated into noise, and consequently there is no gain. Every violinist is not able to produce volume, and in the endeavour to obtain it beauty may be sacrificed.

Players who have heard Wilhelmj or Ysaye have been greatly attracted by the extraordinary volume of the tone produced by these remarkable violinists, but volume is by no means everything, it has very little, if anything, to do with nobility or dignity (as so many violinists suggest), these characteristics being more nearly concerned with the style of rendering the music.

Too much stress should not be placed on volume, as a harsh tone is often the net result. Tone is largely personal and should be developed quite naturally, without ever being forced. Half a dozen violinists playing on the same instrument will all produce a different tone from it, whilst one violinist playing on six different violins will produce a similar character of tone. Physique plays

passes over the strings, and in this connection it is important to remember that the passage of the bow hinges on the movement of the right arm.

Now, it is impossible to discuss the question of tone without mentioning the important part played by the left hand. In addition to stopping the notes the left hand also enters into the argument very considerably by the employment of vibrato.

Let us consider how the mere placing of the finger on the strings in a different part or position will affect tone:—

(a) If we place the whole finger quite flat along the strings and exert as much pressure as we possibly can the tone is lacking in both depth and tensity.

(b) Supposing we release the pressure the tone is even more unsatisfactory. It becomes woolly or flabby and is altogether without character or volume.

(c) We now go to the other extreme and place the uttermost tip of the finger on the string so that the finger nail presses against it. The tone is much more certain and definite in character than previously, but it has become thin, hard and metallic.

(d) The tip of the finger is now placed on the strings as in playing, with a direct downward pressure, and we find that the tone is more satisfactory than when it was placed in the other positions.

(e) By exerting the utmost possible pressure on the tip of the finger, the tone becomes slightly harder, and as we release the unnecessary pressure the tone is once again more normal and less tight.

Now what have we discovered by means of our simple little experiment? :—

(a) That both the quality and the quantity of tone is affected by pressure.

(b) That too much pressure produces a hard tone and too little no tone at all.

(c) That the character of the substance touching the string affects tone.

(d) That the amount of substance touching the string affects tone.

(e) We also know that at a point between the too much and the too little pressure we obtain the most satisfactory tone.

Let us experiment a little further and see how the tone is affected when we employ vibrato.

We fail when we try to produce a tremolo with the whole finger on the strings so we can leave this out of our calculations altogether; but what happens when first the finger nail and then just the tip of the finger are placed on the strings? We find that in each case the tremolo enhances the beauty of the tone to a considerable extent and makes it pulsate with life, but that the finger nail and finger tip tone still retain the same respective characteristics as previously. The finger nail tone is slightly metallic and thin whilst the finger tip tone is resonant and sonorous.

In addition to our other discoveries we now find that stiffness in stopping a note adversely affects tone, and flexibility and looseness have just the opposite effect and increase both the intensity and beauty of the tone.

Let us make one more experiment by varying the rate of our tremolo, and we find that a very quick vibrato produces a rather tight tone, and a very slow one a heavy loose tone. Therefore, our vibrato must be neither too slow nor too quick, with neither too much nor too little pressure, if we are to have a really beautiful tone.

The knowledge gained by these experiments should be applied to our practice.

CHAPTER IV.

ADVICE TO BEGINNERS.

13. BOW DEVELOPMENT OF FIRST IMPORTANCE.

After having described the method of holding the violin, I shall proceed to go through bow technique, for the pupil must always begin to use his bow before the left hand.

As stated at the outset, it is my intention to conclude with finger technique, but I regard this as being far more easily explained (and obtained), and every violinist should be able to develop a good left hand technique provided he possesses sufficient application.

It is a fact that with nearly all amateur violinists and numerous professionals bowing ruins that which the fingers execute. I would far rather see the fingers spoil the result of good bowing, as there would be more hope for the player, but it has never been my good fortune to come across a single instance wherein this fault exists.

From the outset, concentrate on developing your bow, as by doing this you are making the development of finger technique more easy. It is impossible for the beginner to concentrate on both the left and the right hand at the same time. Therefore, if the difficulties that present themselves in bowing are mastered *first*, we are able to give all the attention to the left hand.

Until the bow can be passed over the open strings from point to nut and nut to point in a really satisfactory manner—without scratching, wobbling or whistling—left hand technique should not be embarked upon. There are sufficient troubles in connection with the bow to begin with so do not be too eager to take on fresh worries until you have got rid of the old. In any case, study those exercises which present either difficulties in bowing or fingering—never both. It is only the advanced player who can afford to meet trouble half way—beginners must avoid it.

14. ON SELECTING A MASTER.

As the position in which the violin and bow are held is extremely important, it is essential to begin in the right way. Bad habits acquired early on are easily retained, and it is difficult to get rid of them.

A beginner may overtake a player who has been studying many years because he *began* in the right way. The beginning is everything, so that the choice of a master should be carefully considered.

People are often inclined to say that, " Mr. So-and-so will do for him to begin with, and then " (*when he has acquired no end of faults!*) " he can go to a better master." On the contrary, it is the first lessons that are all-important, and may settle the fate of a would-be violinist. Later—when no progress is made and everything is found to be uninteresting and difficult—the player quickly loses heart and retires from the struggle.

Many violinists began their careers buoyed up by the hope that they would one day become great soloists, and it was only when they found that their hopes were not likely to be quite realised, that they thought of imparting their knowledge to others. They turned to teaching as an after-thought, because they had to in order to supplement an inadequate income. However, as they had little time to give thought to the subject from a teacher's standpoint—though they may have been excellent performers—it is often difficult for them to impart to others the knowledge they acquired fairly easily.

Playing the violin is one thing; teaching it is another.

In these enlightened days a pupil has a right to expect his teacher to be able to tell him something more than the fact that he is "flat" or "sharp" and similar platitudes. Almost any pupil with a good ear should be aware of the fact, and if he is not, he should just be advised to take up an instrument where his shortcomings will not be so apparent.

If one glances back over the past, it will be seen that there have actually been very few great violin teachers, and that practically all the most successful players of the last two centuries have been taught by about a dozen masters.

It is rarely the lot of a teacher (however fine he may be) to turn out more than one or two great violinists, but many teachers have maintained an extraordinary high average with their pupils. It is the average rather than the isolated instance, which points to the fact that a teacher is able to impart his knowledge. The one great pupil would in all probability have played in any circumstances, but it is certain that the remainder, with only average ability, would have done very little if left to themselves. As nine hundred and ninety-nine pupils out of every thousand have no more than average ability, it will be seen that it is essential that the teacher chosen in the first instance should be the best obtainable.

15. ON PURCHASING A VIOLIN.

Having obtained a teacher, the next step is to get a violin and bow. In this case it would certainly be wise to seek the advice of one's teacher; but I would on no account recommend that a great deal of money be paid for a valuable instrument to begin with. Beginners do not understand the value of such an instrument, and they are unable to appreciate its true worth. In any case, the results obtained during the first few months will rarely be more satisfactory because the player is using an old Cremona fiddle. The possession of an old violin should be something to be looked forward to when one has acquired a certain amount of control over one's instrument. Prizes too easily gotten are never appreciated like those hardly won. All that is necessary at the commencement is, that one should have a thoroughly serviceable violin with the correct dimensions, and that it should be properly fitted up. As progress is made, one will hardly be satisfied with an inferior violin; but first endeavour to be worthy of your instrument. It is better that your violin should not be worthy of you, than that you should not be worthy of your violin.

PART II.

CHAPTER V.

THE LEFT SIDE OF THE BODY.

16. HOW THE VIOLIN SHOULD BE HELD.

Now let us begin the practical study of the violin. Much depends on the manner in which the violin is held, but after quite a short time one should be able to accomplish this satisfactorily and without discomfort. Nature gives one no option in the matter of holding the instrument, as she has not provided a support with the exception of the shoulder; therefore, the violin *has* to rest on this. It is gripped quite firmly between the chin or jaw-bone and the left shoulder, and in order that this may be effected, the chin must be turned to the left.* I am anxious

* See " 19. A Few General Hints."

to emphasise this point very strongly, as pupils who have been learning quite a number of years oft-times do not seem to realise the importance of the position of the chin. A small pad placed underneath the violin will considerably facilitate the obtaining of a firm grip, but I have seen numberless players endeavour to hold the violin in front of their body by using a pad the size of a small footstool! If, however, one holds the violin in the correct manner, with the head inclined towards the left shoulder, no difficulty should be experienced in obtaining a firm grip of the instrument, and it should be possible to hold it parallel to the floor without any support from the left hand.

Recently, upon my advising a pupil to use a small pad, he brought to my notice some remarks made by an eminent teacher on this subject in his book on violin playing. They were to the effect that the use of a pad was unnecessary and nothing short of a bad habit, and that a pad helped to destroy the fine vibrations of the instrument. We were told to hold the violin so that the fingers fell perpendicularly on the strings! I could hardly believe this statement until it was shown to me in print, and then I came to the conclusion that the writer's remarks must have been misinterpreted.

We can hold the violin in a million positions so that the finger tips fall perpendicularly on the strings, and we can place them on the strings in this way without holding the violin at all. The violin is held by the chin or jaw-bone in conjunction with some other support, the shoulder, or preferably a pad which does not touch such a large surface of the instrument, and it is obvious that the fingers take no part in holding the violin.

Let us be reasonable—the underneath side of the violin *has* to rest somewhere, and must be supported on something in order that it may be gripped by the chin or jawbone.

The employment of a pad neither makes us play nor prevents our doing so. It is merely an aid to comfort, and in certain cases quite indispensable. Nearly all the violinists with whom I have come in contact during the last 25 years, from Wilhelmj downwards, have found the use of a pad an advantage in enabling them to hold the violin without undue effort, and against the statement that there is a loss of free vibration it may be mentioned that in all probability Wilhelmj had the biggest tone of any violinist that ever lived. If you can hold the violin quite comfortably in the position I have mentioned without a pad—well and good!—there would seem to be no particular reason in your case why you should use one.

Having experimented once or twice to see if it is possible to grip the violin in the manner described, take up your position opposite the violin stand. Do not stand facing the music, but with the left side of your body inclined at an angle of about seventy degrees to the violin stand. The weight of the body should be almost entirely on the left foot. The body should assume an erect position, with the left foot inclined towards the stand. (See Diagram.) The head should then be turned so as to look over the left shoulder, and then, when the violin is placed under-

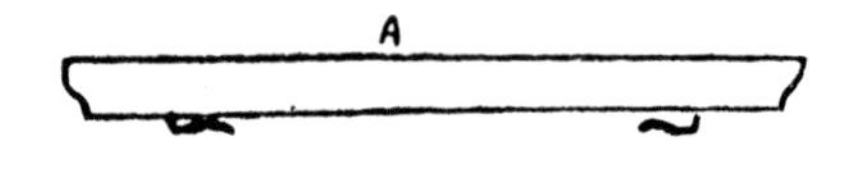

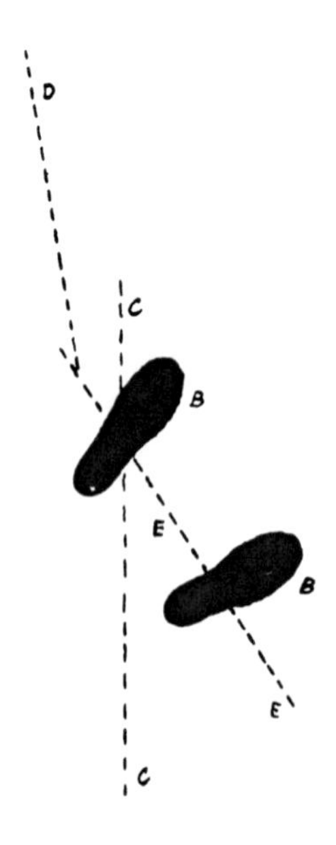

Plan showing approximately the relative angles of (D) violin, (C) head, (E) shoulders, and (B) feet to (A) the music stand.

neath the chin, it should be at right-angles to the music. The right side of the body should be left quite free, and the right foot, which should be slightly in rear of the left, almost parallel to the music stand.

In first taking up one's position in front of the music stand it is essential that one has the correct position of the feet, as otherwise the body will be slewed round directly the violin is gripped by the chin. If the correct position of the feet is maintained, it will be impossible for the body to change its position very considerably. As a matter of fact, no alteration in the position of the body, particularly the shoulders, should take place; therefore watch that the left shoulder is always pointing well towards the music stand, and that both shoulders do not become equidistant from it.

As far as you are able, endeavour to hold the violin in a line with the two shoulders, and directly you begin to play avoid the common fault of dragging it round in front of the body. If you cannot play the violin you can at least have the satisfaction of looking as though you *might*! There is no excuse for standing badly.

17. THE POSITION OF THE THUMB.

The neck of the violin should be placed between the first joint of the thumb and the base of the first finger. The thumb should be held quite naturally, and be kept fairly straight; it then forms a natural V with the base of the first finger, half-way down which the violin rests.

It should be remembered that the thumb is merely there to take the pressure of the fingers, that it should not even support the violin, and that on no account should it give any pressure.

The thumb should not be curled round the neck of the violin, as the loose skin prevents freedom of movement and results in sticking. Sliding, in this case, instead of being smooth and easy, degenerates into a series of uncontrolled jerks.

The exact position of the thumb must vary according to the shape of the hand and length of the fingers. It is unreasonable to be dogmatic on this point. Some players place the thumb slightly behind the first finger, others either opposite or a little in front of it. The point, however, is immaterial so long as the position adopted is quite comfortable to the player.

During sliding, the thumb should move with the hand—as it is part of it. If we think one moment, it is silly to imagine that we can walk upstairs and leave one foot at the bottom. The thumb should not walk up and down the neck as though it were separate from the fingers, as this causes unnecessary movement.

The thumb moves *under* the neck as the higher positions are reached, and it is only when it reaches the end of the neck that it remains stationary, with the tip pressing firmly against it.

The point of the thumb should not be above the finger-board unless it is exceptionally long, and in no case should the neck of the violin be allowed to sink to the bottom of the V at the junction of the thumb and first finger.

18. THE LEFT ELBOW.

The left elbow should be brought well under the violin, but must not rest against the side of the body, as in this event the head of the violin, instead of pointing, as it should, slightly upwards, and at least on a line with the nose of the player, will be dragged down so as to point towards the floor.

I have never seen it stated or explained that there is a movement on the part of the left elbow and that it does not remain stationary. Yet this must be so if the fingers are to retain the same relative position to each string. If the elbow did not move backwards and forwards under the back of the violin, according to which string the fingers were on, the latter would find considerable difficulty in playing on the G string, and be stretched almost straight, whilst they would be curved underneath themselves when playing on the E string. Neither position would be particularly comfortable, or lead to satisfactory results, as in each case the fingers would be cramped in their movement. It is important to remember, therefore, that the elbow is more towards the sound post (the E string) whilst playing the G string, and that it moves slightly away from it as the fingers play on the higher strings.

19. A FEW GENERAL HINTS.

The beginner finds that he cannot hold the violin in its correct position for any considerable length of time, and it would be better for him to assume the position, correct any faults that he may observe, and then rest for a moment. In a minute or so he will be able to repeat the movement, and so on, each time correcting any errors that may have been made.

The violin should not be held for too lengthy periods to begin with, as it leads to physical fatigue, and consequently mental relaxation.

Practically every player uses a chin-rest, which considerably facilitates the holding of the instrument. Chin-rests can be obtained in all patterns to suit every player's comfort.

Nearly all violinists find it more comfortable to place the underside of the jawbone on the chin-rest rather than the point of the chin, and this often tends to a firmer and more comfortable grip being obtained. At the same time, it should not lead to the head being pushed forward or to one side, as, apart from the discomfort of such a position, the result is that it looks unnatural and awkward.

The body should remain quite still during practice, and should not, on any account, be swayed from side to side, while the head should remain erect, and, if anything, slightly back, so that the eyes may look upward.

The height of the stand should also be considered. It must not be too low, as this necessitates bending down in order to see the music; better for it to be too high, which makes it more necessary to look up with the head and body erect whilst playing.

CHAPTER VI.

THE RIGHT SIDE OF THE BODY (THE BOW ARM).

20. HOW TO HOLD THE BOW.

PERHAPS the greatest difficulty is experienced by the beginner when he first endeavours to get a satisfactory grip of the bow. He either places his hand half-way round the nut, or endeavours to hold it with the finger tips just perched on the stick.

A satisfactory tone cannot be obtained unless the grip on the bow is perfectly balanced. It should be realised at once that to hold the bow in the correct manner is a much more subtle and difficult thing to accomplish than to hold the violin. The grip must be one which allows perfect freedom of movement while giving the greatest amount of control.

Plate II.

HOW TO HOLD THE BOW.

Explanation.

Note the following points:—

a. Position of tip of thumb.

b. Side of thumb touches stick and centre of tip the nut.

c. First joint of thumb bent almost at right angles.

d. First joint of thumb inclined towards point of bow.

e. Tip practically opposite to second finger.

f. Position of first three fingers *round* stick (not on top).

g. Tip of the fourth finger resting on top of stick slightly behind the third finger.

h. All the fingers lying comfortably together so as to centralise the control.

i. Note line of the knuckles and general curve of fingers.

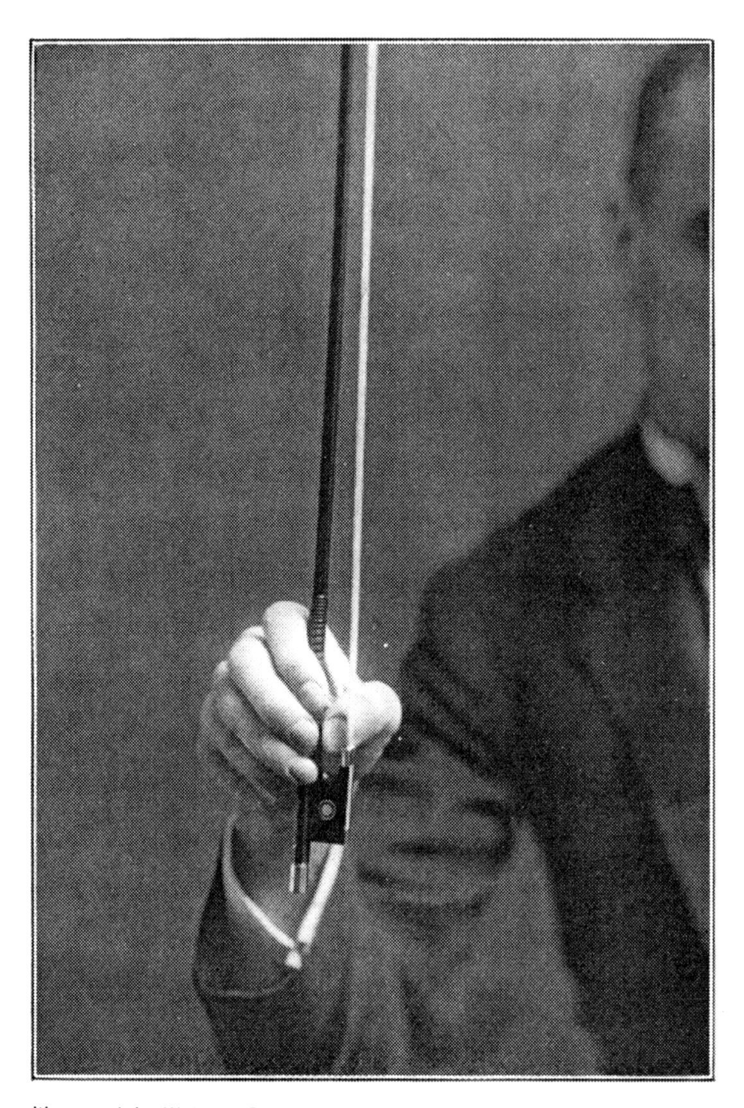

Photograph by Wykeham.]

PLATE II

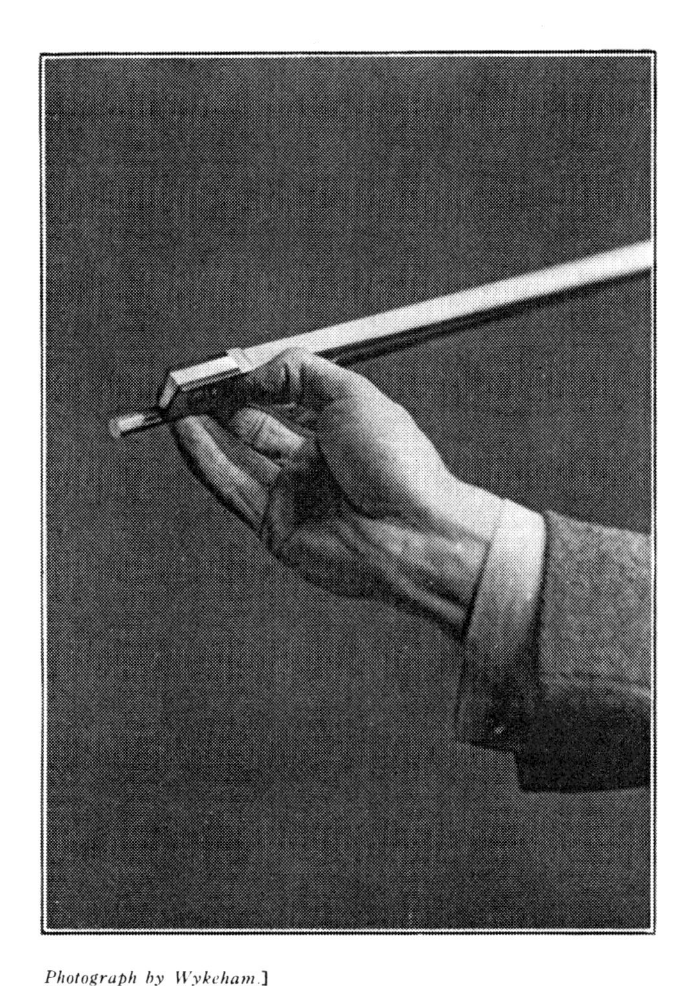

Photograph by Wykeham.]

PLATE IIA.

Another view of hand showing correct position of fingers and thumb. (Compare Plates II., IIA. and IIB. with Plates IIC. and IID.

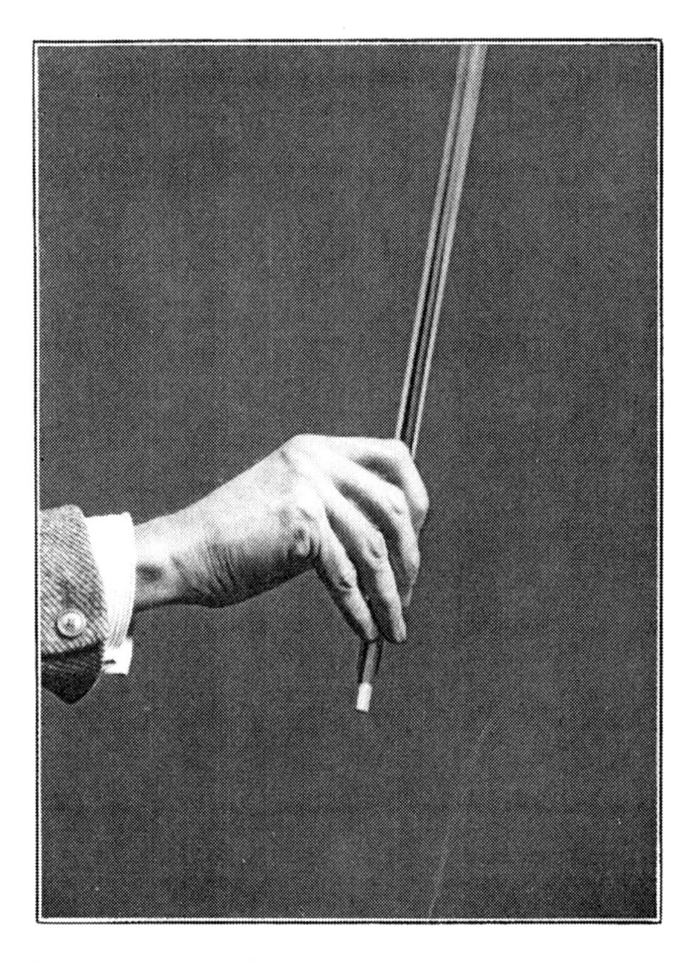

Photograph by Wykeham.]

PLATE IIB.

Showing correct position of fingers on stick.

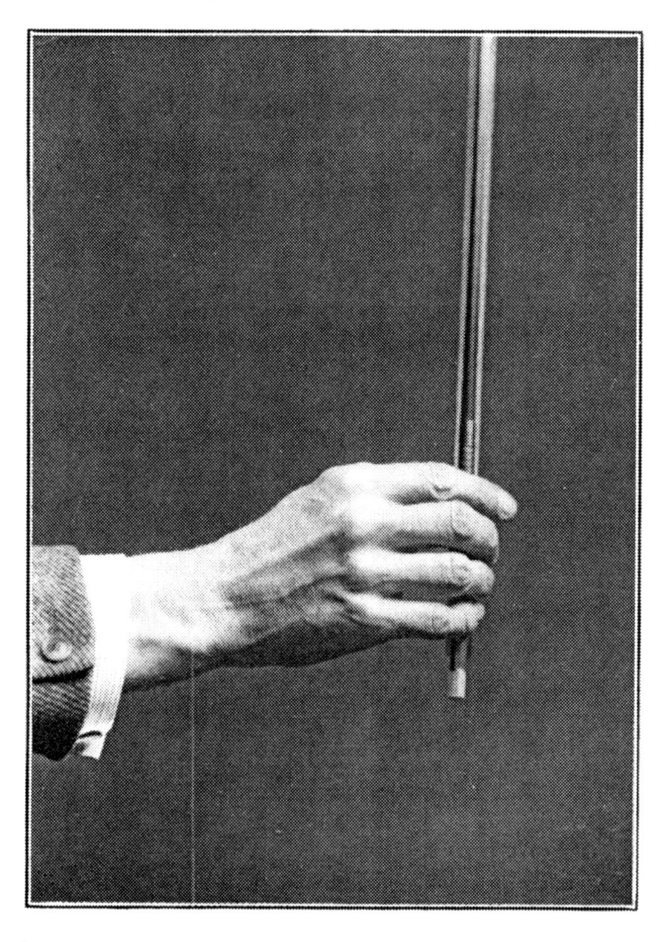

Photograph by Wykeham.]

PLATE IIc.

Showing incorrect position of fingers and hand in relation to the stick.

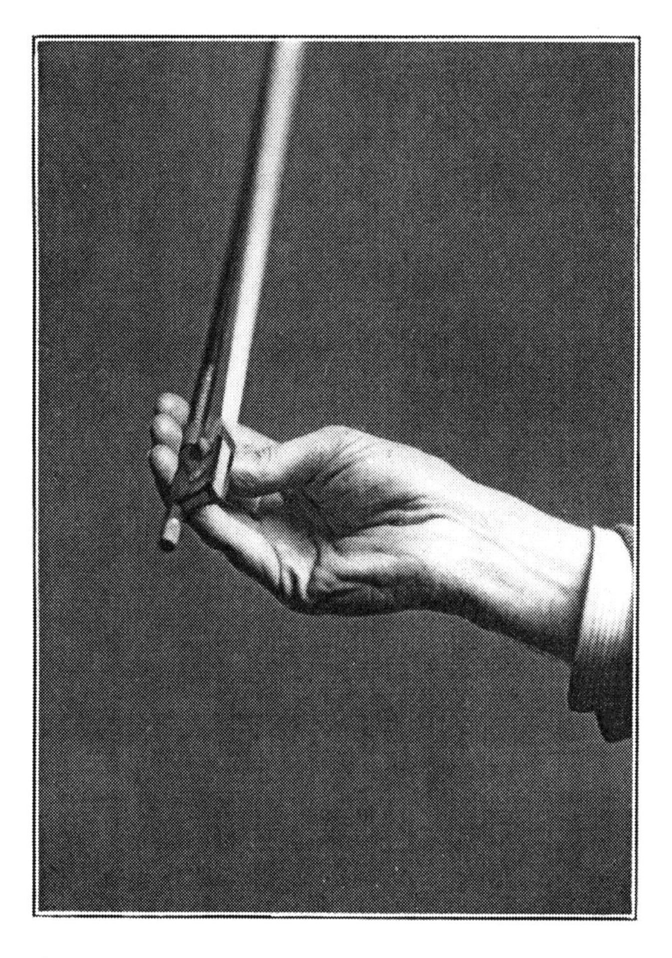

Photograph by Wykeham.]

PLATE IID.

Another view showing incorrect position of thumb and fingers.

The thumb joint should be turned outwards (viz., bent almost at right angles), so as to point away from the knuckles, and slightly in the direction of the tip of the bow.

Endeavour to pick up a needle between your thumb and two middle fingers; then you have approximately the position in which the fingers and thumb should be placed *round* the stick.

Having turned your thumb well out, place the tip at the base of the nut (not in the frog); *half the tip of the thumb will then be resting on the stick, and the remainder on the point of the nut.* As stated above, the thumb joint should be inclined slightly towards the tip of the bow. There will then be a direct *downward* grip on the bow.

The first finger should lie along the stick with that portion of it above the first joint curling, as it were, *just round the stick*, the latter will then lie between the first and second joints of the first finger. The second and third fingers should rest over the stick in like manner, but they should not be allowed to slide too far round the stick so as to meet the tip of the thumb. The tip of the fourth finger will merely be placed on the top of the stick. The hold should be one of ease and comfort without stiffness.

When the fingers and thumb are in the position described, the tip of the second finger should be about opposite to the tip of the thumb, and *all* the finger joints slightly bent, with the possible exception of the fourth finger.

The second and third fingers with the assistance of the thumb supply the main hold on the stick, while the first finger is chiefly instrumental in applying pressure, and the fourth finger in relieving it wherever necessary.

The whole hand should be inclined towards the stick (that is, towards the first finger); the first finger should press decidedly against the wood, while the tip of the fourth finger should be in a tense (not stiff) condition, so as to take the weight of the bow off the strings whenever necessary.

On no account should the fingers be cramped too much together, neither should they be placed too far apart or a strained position adopted.

It should be possible, early on, to hold the bow quite naturally. Pick it up on every occasion, and adopt the correct position, when the feeling of the stick and a sense of its balance will come to you.

Having obtained a correct hold of both the violin and bow, rest for a moment, placing them out of your hands; then keep repeating the performance until you find that you can take them up quite naturally and easily, almost without having to consider in what manner you do so. By constantly practising this you will obtain the position without effort, but until you are sure that you have progressed thus far correctly, do not proceed to make any movement with the right arm.

21. ON BOWING.

You are now quite comfortable when you take the violin and bow in your hands, and, as you are able to assume a correct position of the body in relation to the violin stand, let us go on to the next step, which is to pass the bow over the strings.

Try and realise that this is your first lesson in voice production. You are going to speak for the first time in a fresh language; therefore, do not be disappointed with your early efforts. To begin with, your tone will not be altogether satisfactory; but do not be discouraged by this. You will learn to articulate naturally in quite a short time provided you do nothing without *thinking first* of what you are about to undertake. If you blindly place the bow on the strings as most beginners do, the result will be terrifying, and it will remain so as long as you pursue your present method of procedure.

It is quiet thought and understanding which will ultimately lead you to success. Do not look for *results* immediately; these will come automatically *in time*, but the more you expect of your early attempts the less likely are you to make satisfactory progress.

Blessed indeed is he that expecteth nothing when beginning to play the violin!

Take care that you do the movements in a correct manner, and in time you will be sure to succeed.

Do not attempt to place the fingers of the left hand on the strings and add to the medley of noise already produced by the plain open strings until you can pass the bow satisfactorily from one end to the other without scratching or breaking the tone. When you have succeeded in drawing the bow smoothly from tip to nut and nut to tip then, and then only, should you attempt to place your first finger on the strings.

The violin is speechless except in pizzicato, so that the bow is as much a part of violin tone as the violin itself. Perhaps I may be forgiven for repeating that which I have stated elsewhere (as I am unable to make myself more clear): "Physically, the bow is the productive agent; but mentally, it should be something more. This mental difference I consider very important, as, if the violin is considered as being the entire voice, there is a mental and unconscious transference of the control and everything connected with the voice to the left hand—which has practically nothing to do with the voice or its control beyond the mere stopping of the notes—and the bow is only too often left to take care of itself. This is especially the case with beginners. Therefore, I look upon the individual as being the productive agent, and the violin and bow together as the voice."

22 THE MOVEMENT OF THE RIGHT ARM.

In order that the stroke may be executed satisfactorily, I shall now describe the different movements that the arm executes in the course of the bow's passage from one end to the other.

If we employ the whole arm when only an inch or two of the bow is to be moved, the effect will be disastrous. The arm itself is sub-divided into certain divisions; therefore, for a small portion of the bow we only require to move a small portion of the arm or wrist. For whole bows we employ the whole arm. Small strokes require the use of a delicate movement of the wrist and fingers, larger strokes the wrist and fingers in conjunction with the fore-arm, until for whole bows the whole arm from shoulder to finger tips is brought into use.

We will assume that the player is holding the bow as previously described, and that he has now placed the tip of it lightly against the A string. In this position, the elbow should not drop against the side of the body, but if anything it should be slightly higher than the stick of the bow. This will ensure the first finger pressing firmly against it.

The weight of the arm should be kept off the stick in order that pressure may be applied or released whenever required. The right arm should be tense and very decidedly under control. There is always a strong tendency with beginners to allow the arm to flop. This leads to a dead tone, whereas if the weight of the arm is removed the bow—and consequently the tone—remains full of elasticity. The weight of the bow should *at no time* be allowed to rest of its own accord on the strings, as this can never lead to a

Plate III.

SHOWING POSITION OF THUMB AND LEFT ARM.

Explanation.

a. The thumb is straight and does not bend round the neck.

b. The thumb slightly behind the first finger in order to avoid gripping.

c. Wrist and forearm form practically a straight line.

d. Elbow well away from the body.

(For position of fingers on strings see frontispiece.)

Photograph by Wykeham.]

PLATE III

satisfactory result. Pressure is applied at the point; when the nut is reached the pressure is taken off and the weight of the bow removed from the strings.

So many players never get away from the middle of the bow because they neither apply nor take off pressure. They merely allow the bow to rest on the strings. Fair results can be obtained only so long as one remains in the middle of the bow, but directly the nut is reached the scratching is truly appalling, while at the point there is no tone at all. Therefore, the condition of the upper and forearm should be tense and not relaxed.

23. FROM POINT TO MIDDLE.

Having placed the tip of the bow on the strings, move it gradually upwards until the middle is reached. In order to accomplish this, it is necessary to change the position of the forearm and wrist. The upper-arm remains almost stationary, though not altogether so, as there is a slight backward movement of the elbow in order to allow the

Plate IV.

POSITION OF RIGHT ARM WHEN POINT OF BOW IS ON THE STRINGS.

(Left Hand in Third Position.)

Explanation.

a. Note position of right hand and fingers.

b. Fingers and hand inclined towards stick.

c. First three fingers curved, the fourth straightened.

d. Wrist lowered.

e. Right elbow slightly in advance of shoulder and away from body.

f. Easy lines of arms and fingers of both hands.

g. General easy posture.

h. Base of left hand touching violin in third position.

i. Note height and inclination of violin and direction and position of head.

Photograph by Wykeham.]

PLATE IV

bow to remain parallel to the bridge. If the upper-arm did not move at all, the bow would necessarily be forced away from the body (and therefore over the fingerboard) on account of the changed position of the forearm. While the forearm is moving upwards the wrist must gradually rise until it is almost in a line with the forearm by the time the middle of the bow is reached. We shall then have the forearm and wrist in a line parallel with the strings of the violin. The hand and fingers will retain the same position in relation to the bow that they did at the commencement of the stroke; the only difference will be that they have moved nearer the violin than previously. Throughout this movement the bow should remain parallel with the bridge, and should neither get nearer to it nor closer to the fingerboard.

Having reached the middle of the bow and observed the position of the arm in order to ensure that it is correct, repeat the action again and again until you are certain that you have mastered it, always commencing at the point, and not attempting to move the bow backwards until the up-stroke from the point to the middle has been accomplished successfully. One of the chief faults that occurs is a variation in the height of the elbow. It will be found that the elbow moves either upwards or closer to the body, and however imperceptible this movement, it should be immediately checked.

When you can reach the middle of the bow in the manner described, then endeavour to go back to your original position at the point, leaving the bow this time *on* the strings. You will once again find that in reversing the movement the elbow either drops or rises; but this is the chief point to be observed. The only alteration that takes place in the position of the elbow is that it moves slightly backwards, but it should remain at practically the same height from the floor and the same relative distance from the body as when the movement of the bow was begun.

Criticise every movement you make, and you will greatly facilitate your progress. Observe that at all times when the centre of the bow is reached the strings of the violin, the forearm, the upper-arm and the stick of the bow are very nearly parallel to each other.

The shape of this " parallelogram " will vary somewhat with each individual according to variation in the length of the arm.

24. FROM MIDDLE TO NUT.

So far, the upper-arm has played a very small part in making the stroke. It has merely endeavoured to get out of the way, as it were, so as not to push the bow towards the finger-board. Now, however, we are going to employ it to the full extent, in addition to the wrist and forearm, which have previously done all the work. Unless the weight of the upper-arm is taken off the strings, it will become apparent that the upper-arm is rather heavy and somewhat of an encumbrance.

Let us place the bow on the strings once again at the middle, observing that we have our parallelogram. Continue the upward movement of the forearm and the rising of

Plate V.

POSITION OF RIGHT ARM AT MIDDLE OF BOW.

(Left Hand in Fifth Position.)

Explanation.

The photograph illustrates the position of the right arm shortly before the middle of the bow is reached. For the purpose of comparison, lines have been inserted to show the position at the middle of the bow.

It should be noted that the elbow moves back and the wrist rises until it is almost in a straight line with the forearm, which is about parallel with the violin.

The position of the right hand and fingers, with the fourth, straight remains relatively the same as in Plate IV.

Note the position of the left hand and fingers well above the strings in the fifth position. The hand has also begun to move round the violin.

Photograph by Wykeham.]

PLATE V

the wrist, and allow the elbow to come forward. The elbow will therefore be moving slightly round and across the chest of the player.

The whole of the upper-arm, forearm and wrist movement from the point to the tip of the bow takes place in one plane. *It is merely one movement*, each portion of the arm being employed whenever necessary. The wrist simply rises at the point nearest your body in order that the hand and fingers may retain the same relationship towards the bow, and the forearm and upper-arm "give" just sufficiently to allow the bow to be moved until the nut reaches the strings.

When this portion of the movement has been completed satisfactorily, then, and then only, should the whole bow be taken from the point to the nut. Commence with up bows, always stopping in the middle to check your position, and having ascertained that so far you are correct, continue the movement to its completion.

When the up bows have been mastered, down bows may be attempted; but once again,

Plate VI.

POSITION OF RIGHT ARM AT NUT OF BOW.

(Left Hand in Eighth Position.)

Explanation.

Note that the right elbow has swung *forward* and not upward. The hand and fingers have retained the same relationship towards the stick as at the commencement of the stroke. Compare this with Plates IV. and V. The fourth finger on the bow is still straight, as no finger flexion has yet taken place, the bow being on the strings, about three inches away from the nut.

Observe position of the left hand and fingers, the former well round and the latter directly above the violin.

Photograph by Wykeham.]

PLATE VI

pause in the middle to check your parallelogram. When you are assured that your positions are correct, you may proceed to move the bow its complete length, checking it at either end before commencing the next stroke either upwards or downwards, as the case may be.

Only a portion of the hair touches the strings, so that the stick is inclined towards the finger-board. The bow should not turn from side to side while the stroke is being made, but retain the same relative angle towards the strings from the point to the nut. In order that tensity may be maintained, the stick should always remain well above the hair. If the bow is inclined too much towards the strings, it will be found that the wood usually touches them when any pressure is applied at the middle.

KEY TO DIAGRAM I.

A. This merely represents a fixture to which our appliance is attached.

B. Screw connecting E with A.

C. Screw connecting F with E.

D. Screw connecting G with F.

E, F, G represent flat strips of wood joined together for the purpose of illustrating the movements made by the right arm during the course of the stroke.

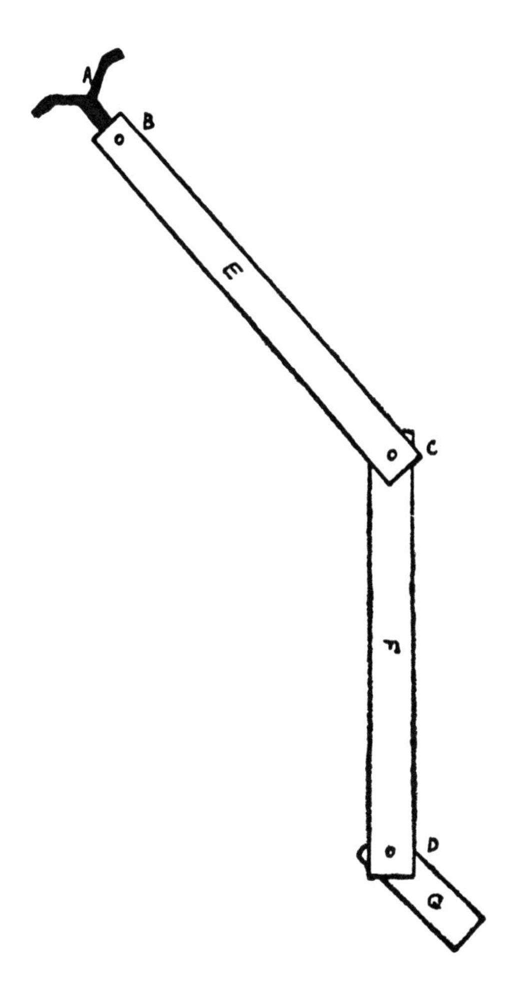

DIAGRAM I.

DIAGRAM II.

This shows our simple appliance in position.

A. Let us take this as representing the body of the player, which should remain stationary. B. The shoulder. E. The upper-arm. C. The elbow. F. The forearm. D. The wrist. G. The hand and fingers. H. The line made by the bow during the course of the stroke. J. An imaginary line through the centre of the violin. For the purposes of illustration let us say that this represents the position of the arm when the point of the bow is placed on the strings.

In Diagram II. I have added two dotted lines, J and H representing respectively an imaginary line through the centre of the violin and that made by the bow during the course of the stroke. In addition, I have placed our appliance so that it represents very nearly the position of the player's bow arm when playing at the point. Let us imagine that A is fixed to some definite support so that only the joints at B, C, and D can be moved, and that G can merely be worked up and down the line H.

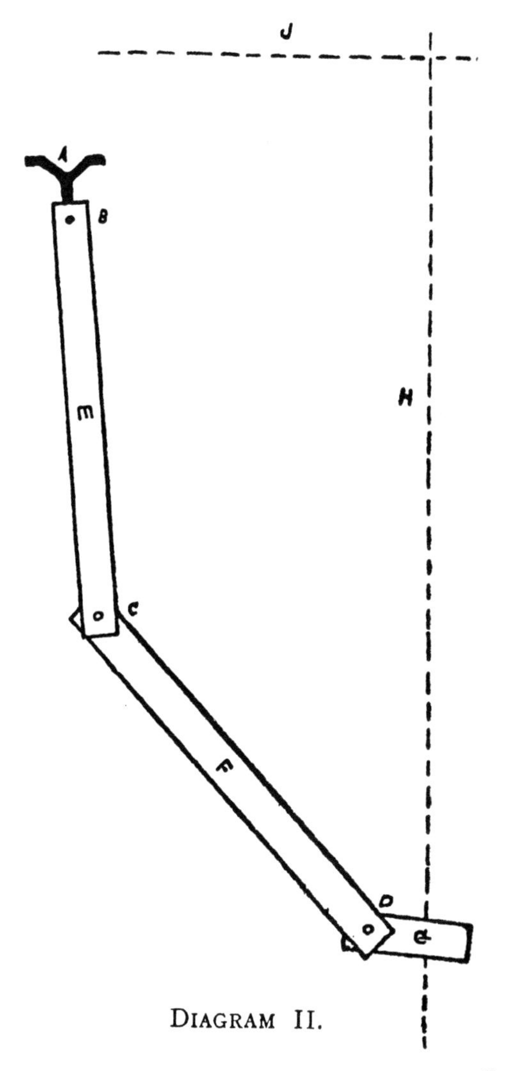

DIAGRAM II.

CHAPTER VII.

25. THE MOVEMENT OF THE RIGHT ARM ILLUSTRATED.

In order to explain the movements made by the right arm during the course of a stroke, I have drawn a simple illustration in Diagram I., which shows three pieces of wood screwed together at B, C and D, the whole of which is hanging from a support at A. I usually find that considerable difficulty is experienced by players in understanding my meaning, when I ask them to move their arm in one plane. The three pieces of wood which we have taken for the purpose of our illustration are quite flat, and when they are screwed together at B, C and D, it is only possible for them to move in one plane.

Now let us proceed to Diagram III. It will be noticed that the position is changed so as to represent the bow when the middle rests on the strings. It will be seen that the two pieces of wood representing the forearm and hand have moved up, until they are approximately in a straight line, and in order to allow the increased length of the forearm on account of its now being placed at right angles to the bow, it will be observed that the elbow has moved slightly backwards, and in consequence the upper-arm from the shoulder has had to make a similar movement. Be careful to note that the hand retains the same relative position towards the line of the bow (and the violin) as it did when the stroke was begun. In addition, we now have approximately the parallelogram of which I have previously spoken—the fore-arm is practically parallel to the strings, and the upper-arm nearly parallel to the line of the bow. I wish it to be understood that these angles are by no means exact right-

DIAGRAM III.

This represents the position of the right arm when the middle of the bow rests on the strings. (The dotted lines are for the purposes of comparison with the position when at the point of the bow.)

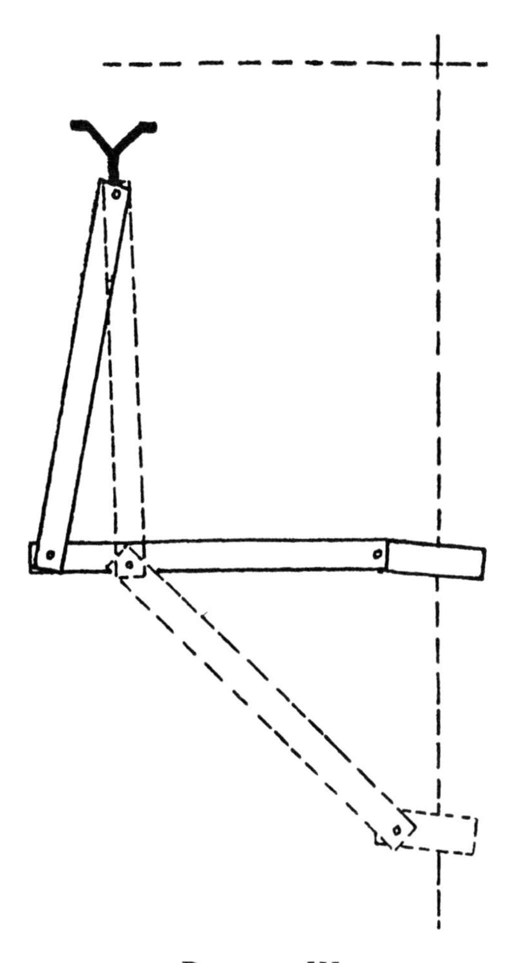

DIAGRAM III.

Plate VII.

INCORRECT POSITION.

Explanation.

Note the following faults:—

Right elbow dropped towards body, wrist too high, and hand and fingers turned away from stick instead of inclining towards it. Compare the lines of the right arm with the two positions shown in Plate V. The middle of the bow is resting on the strings, and the right elbow has remained forward and close into the body instead of moving backwards and remaining at its original height The position should be as shown by the lines sketched in Plate V. The tip of the bow also has a tendency to move round the neck of the player owing to the hand being pushed forward. The position of the left hand is entirely wrong. Here the fingers are resting on higher notes than in Plate VI., yet the wrist remains in a retarded position owing to the hand being insufficiently raised above the finger-board. The wrist is actually *behind* the thumb, which can be seen in Plate VI. Compare the position of the wrist in this and the previous Plate. It will be seen that the whole attitude is cramped, uncomfortable, and altogether lacking in ease and control.

Photograph by Wykeham.]

PLATE VII

angles, and that in any case they would vary slightly with each individual player, on account of the fact that some of us have longer arms than others. But in the main, this description will serve for general purposes.

For the conclusion of the stroke from the middle to the point, let us go to Diagram IV. The two previous positions are shown for the purpose of comparison. If we compare the position of the imaginary elbow joint when we were playing in the middle of the bow and now, we shall see that the elbow has come forward very considerably, which has made it possible for the wrist joint to rise until the nut of the bow has reached the strings. Once again I would draw the reader's attention to the fact that the hand has retained the *same relative position* to the bow throughout the stroke.

I hope that this simple illustration will have made my meaning quite clear, and the reader should no longer find any difficulty in understanding what is intended by "Moving in one plane."

Diagram IV.

Showing the position of the arm when the nut of the bow is on the strings. (The dotted lines are for the purposes of comparison with the two previous positions at the point and middle of the bow.)

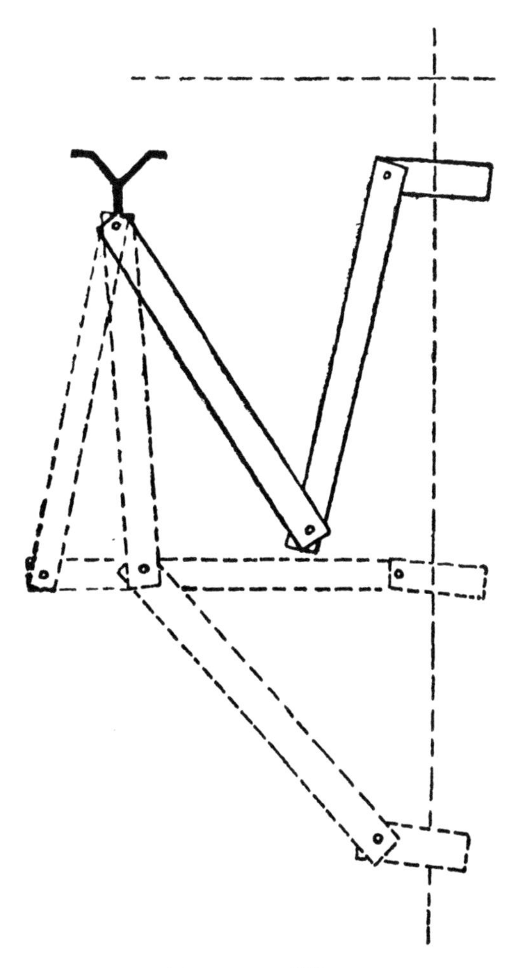

DIAGRAM IV.

26. THE ANGLE OF THE RIGHT ARM WHEN PLAYING ON DIFFERENT STRINGS.

We now come to Diagram V., which shows the bridge of a violin, and in order to illustrate the angle made by the bow when playing on each string, I have drawn a straight line across each one.

In addition to representing the line along which the bow moves, these lines also represent the planes in which the bow arm works. Therefore, whilst playing on the E string, all the movements made by the right arm should take place within the line marked "E." The same remarks apply to the A, D and G strings. It will therefore be seen that there are four different planes in which the right arm moves.

Should we play a portion of one bow on the A string, and then the remainder on the D or G string, the whole arm from the shoulder moves into the desired plane, and no movement of any one portion of the arm should take place in any other plane. It

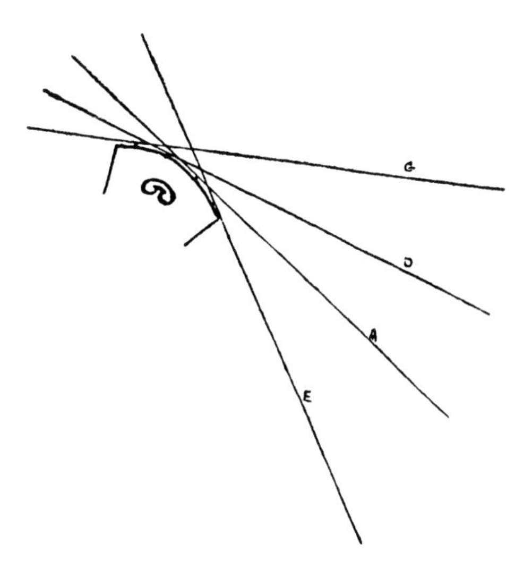

Diagram V.

Showing the angle of the right arm (which should coincide with the line of the bow) when playing on the different strings.

will be seen that when we are playing on the G string the arm must necessarily be almost parallel with the floor, and that as we get to the higher strings the arm drops, until by the time the E string is reached it is *almost* by the side of the body.

Let us place the point of the bow on the E string, and then without playing any note merely raise the arm until the point touches the A string, moving the whole arm direct from the shoulder, taking care to see that no individual movement is made by either the hand, wrist or elbow. The bow-arm has moved from one position to another, and in each case it should retain the same *relative* position to the bow. Great care will have to be exercised in observing that the elbow makes the same movement as the middle of the bow. The tendency is always to leave the elbow in its original position and to raise the right hand, which causes the bow to turn from the side of the hair to the flat.

I have explained that there are four separate planes in which the bow moves, and in addition to this, there are three others which we use when playing double stopping. While the bow remains on one or two strings so long does the arm remain in one plane, and no movement of any portion of the arm or wrist takes place outside that plane.

Once again, I must refer to the antiquated idea that the bow-arm should remain glued to the side of the body. After what I have said, only a moment's thought is necessary to show the fallacy of such an idea; so do not endeavour to play the violin with a book held under your right arm.

Before leaving the stroke I should like to explain once again which part of the arm should be used for each division of the bow. from the point to the middle, the forearm and wrist, with a slight backward movement of the elbow; the wrist rises until the hand and forearm are practically in a straight line, which should be about parallel to the finger-board. From the middle to the nut, the whole arm from the shoulder is brought into use. The wrist and forearm continue to move upwards, during the course of which the elbow comes *forward*, following the nut

Plate VIII.

POSITION AND HEIGHT OF RIGHT ARM WHILST PLAYING ON E STRING.

Explanation.

Note the line of right arm, with elbow well away from the body. The whole position is one of ease and comfort allied to perfect control. The hand is inclined towards the bow, and it should be observed that the knuckles of the right hand are not depressed, which remark applies to their position at all times. Notice incorrect position of fingers of left hand, and compare with correct position in Plate IX.

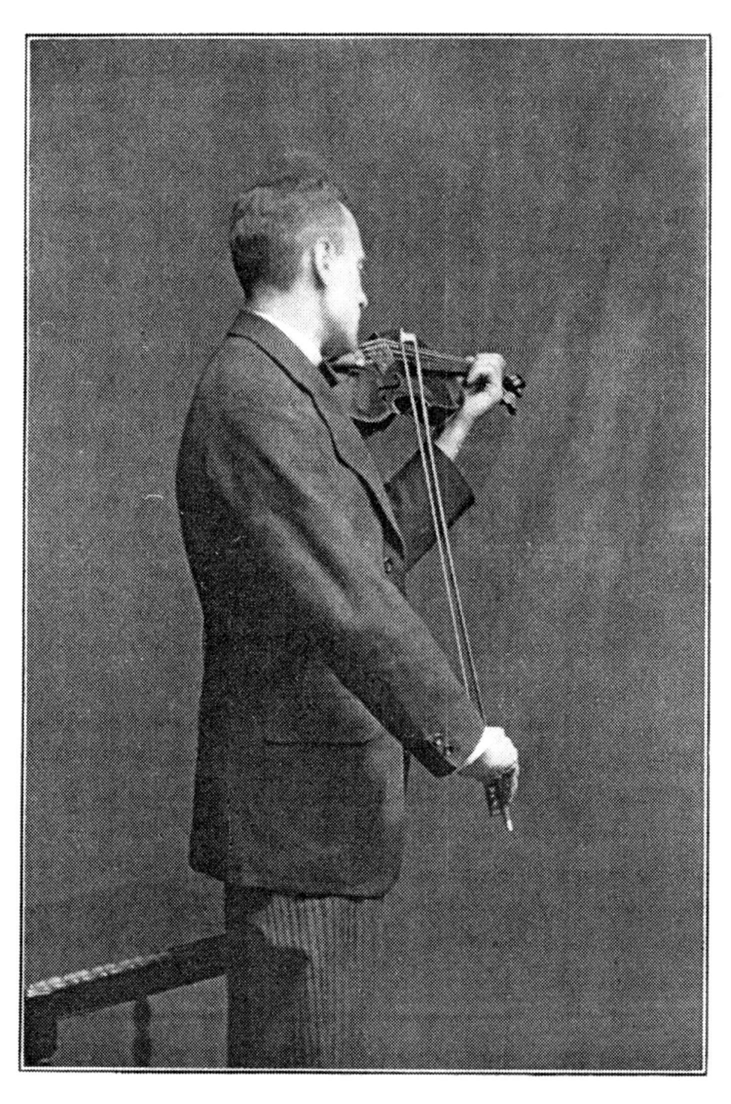

Photograph by Wykeham.]

PLATE VIII

of the bow, as it were. The whole of the movements take place in one plane, and no portion of the arm makes a movement in any other plane.

CHAPTER VIII.

27. THE COMPLETE STROKE.

So far, I have only dealt with half bows and whole bows, which have been accomplished by movements of the wrist, forearm, elbow and upper-arm; but now we come to what is, perhaps, the most important part of the stroke—a finger flexion at the nut.

We know quite well the difficulty that is experienced in playing satisfactorily at the nut of the bow, and how difficult it is to avoid scratching. If we wish to employ two bows together (up and down) and merely used a movement of the *whole* arm, there would be a perceptible break between the upward and downward stroke, as such a cumbersome piece of machinery would have to be brought to a standstill before it could commence the return journey.

Let us liken our whole arm movement to a railway train proceeding in a northward direction. Supposing that it suddenly required to return the way it came; it would be necessary for the engine to come to a standstill, and then actually to get up speed again in order that it might proceed in a southward direction. The same idea applies to the movement of the right arm. There is a perceptible stop between the upward and downward movements, and in order to get over this we check the arm movement just before the completion of the stroke and allow the fingers and wrist to move the last two inches of the bow over the strings. The finger movement acts as "buffers," and prevents the jerk that would otherwise take place if they were not employed. They are much more delicate machinery than the whole arm, and it is possible for them to effect the completion of the stroke and the return journey without any perceptible break in the tone.

Players who are unable to use their fingers and wrist in the correct manner always find that the downward stroke is commenced by a very perceptible " bite " on the strings, which causes an unnecessarily harsh tone. If, however, in order to avoid this, the pressure of the bow upon the strings is released, tensity is lost, and a certain monotony is produced in the playing. The wrist may be quite free, but it helps very little if the fingers do not also play their part—just as it would be useless for the arm to be free and the wrist stiff.

By freedom I do not intend to convey " floppiness "; the bow can only be moved satisfactorily over the strings when the whole arm is in a tensely controlled condition. It is this tense control that the beginner finds so difficult to obtain, but which in the end leads to the attainment of a perfect legato.

Perhaps I should here explain that legato is executed by moving in one plane, and staccato and all other " fancy " bowings by working in slightly different planes.

There are definite rules for the execution of each; and as legato and staccato are opposite effects, it is impossible to execute them both in the same manner.

28.—FINGER FLEXION AND WRIST-MOVEMENT.

Most players have observed that all well-known performers give the bow a sort of "flick" when the nut is reached in order to bring it back on the return journey. This movement is executed at such lightning speed that it is almost imperceptible, and it was only after a number of years' quiet observation that I could explain to pupils what actually took place.

Sometimes this "finger flexion" is acquired by laborious practice or by observing one's teacher, but it is a lengthy and tiring process, and in the end it does not get any farther—if as far—as would be the case if the movement were explained at the outset in detail.

Let us place the bow on the strings to

PLATE IX.

POSITION AND HEIGHT OF RIGHT ARM WHILST PLAYING ON G STRING.

EXPLANATION.

It should be noted that the arm and bow together have changed their height, and that *no* portion of the arm has moved independently. The height of the whole arm has been changed direct from the shoulder, and it is now almost parallel to the floor. Note that the fourth finger remains straight, and observe easy position of fingers of left hand.

Photograph by Wykeham.]

PLATE IX

within two or three inches of the nut. The forearm and upper-arm should remain stationary, having completed their movement; but if we continue the movement of the hand from the wrist it will be found that this merely has the effect of bringing the bow over the left shoulder, and the tone produced will not be very gratifying. If, however, we draw the little finger towards the palm of the right hand, and the second and third fingers a proportionate amount, at the same time bringing the bow with them, we find that the wrist or hand movement is counteracted by the motion of the fingers, and that the bow proceeds to complete the last two inches of the stroke whilst retaining the same relative position towards the strings.

In order to move the fingers in the manner described it is necessary that the thumb joint should gradually be bent outwards—a little more than is usually the case.

In the downward movement the thumb and fingers will resume their previous position (the normal one), the little finger becoming quite straight once again.

PLATE X.

POSITION OF RIGHT HAND AND FINGERS PREPARATORY TO FINGER FLEXION.

EXPLANATION.

The fourth finger remains straight, the bow resting on the strings about two or three inches away from the nut. It should be noticed that the position corresponds to that in Plate VI., and the same observations apply.

Photograph by Wykeham.]

PLATE X

This flexion of the fingers and thumb is perhaps the most important part of the stroke, and it is almost entirely absent from the ordinary amateur's equipment. Unfortunately for many players, it is one of the essentials of violin playing.

In addition to doing away with scratching and clumsiness, it has the effect of counteracting stiffness, and consequently leads to ease in playing.

The finger flexion keeps the bow perfectly under control, and it will be seen that no wrist movement is of the slightest account unless the fingers also play their part. Flexibility of the thumb and finger joints is essential.

In order to make the above a little more clear, let me recapitulate some of the points.

The tips of the fourth finger and thumb will begin to turn inwards and a little upwards, slightly towards the palm of the hand as the latter (and consequently the bow) rises. This will cause the second and third fingers to bend slightly also. The first finger merely acts as a pivot upon which the movement revolves. The hand having arrived at its highest point, both it and the fingers begin to move backwards, reversing the movement, the fingers beginning to do so first. During the upward movement the little finger and thumb will assist by releasing pressure (giving) and by bending outwards; while in the downward stroke they will help by exerting pressure and forcing the bow downwards, consequently away from the palm of the hand. In the up-stroke the fingers draw the nut of the bow (the screw) towards the palm of the hand, and in the down-stroke force the screw away from it.

29. THE FUNCTIONS OF THE FINGERS.

The reason will now be seen why I stated that in holding the bow the fingers should not overlap the stick beyond the first joint, as if this is done it is impossible to utilise the services of the other joints. In addition to merely retaining a hold on the stick, each finger has a separate function to execute.

The first finger applies pressure, the second and third, together with the thumb, support the stick, while the little finger relieves the pressure when playing at the nut and keeps the bow from weighing too heavily on the strings. The whole of the fingers (that is, if the stick is held correctly) maintain tensity while the bow is passing over the strings. All the fingers work together in order to ensure perfect control; even the second and third fingers, together with the thumb, assist to apply and remove pressure, thus helping the first and fourth fingers to perform their duties and at all times to retain the *balance* of the stick.

30. THE FOURTH FINGER.

So many players seem to discard their fourth finger, and one notices that whenever there is little or no control the player appears to be under the impression that he can hold the bow more perfectly with three fingers than with four.

No violinist had a finer bow than Sarasate, who always used all four fingers whilst playing. As a matter of fact, the fourth finger assists in the development of bow control in the first instance more effectively, perhaps, than any other finger. It should, therefore, remain touching the stick at all times, with the possible exception of upward and downward staccato bowings. If you are an experienced violinist it may be that you can upon occasions dispense with the use of your little finger, but until you have learnt how to use it do not despise it on account of its size! You have only four fingers and a thumb on each hand with which to work, and you will find that they are none too many for the purpose for which you require them. In any case, learn how to employ them and to what use they may be put, before you decide to discard them.

One of the chief reasons why so many players do not keep the tip of their little finger resting on the bow lies in the fact that they do not lower the wrist sufficiently at the point in order to enable them to do so. By taking the fourth finger off the bow they do not correct their error, but make it rather more apparent. No great teacher has ever advocated discarding the use of the little finger, but as bow technique has developed teachers have more and more emphasised the importance of employing it to the fullest possible degree.

CHAPTER IX.

31. WRIST MOVEMENT WHEN CROSSING OVER THE STRINGS.

(*Rotary movement of the hand.*)

UP to the present we have merely played on one string, but we shall find that our difficulties are considerably increased directly we endeavour to play short bows on different strings.

I will assume that we have now obtained control over the wrist and finger movement, and that we desire to cross from the D to the A string in short bows, either at the nut or the middle of the bow. We shall execute the stroke on, say, the D string by means of the wrist and finger flexion previously described, and then, without moving the forearm or upper-arm, merely turn the whole *hand* slightly downwards so that the nut is brought a little nearer to the butt of the violin when the hair will rest on the A string. Only a very slight movement of the hand is necessary in order to effect this, as will be seen by observing Diagram V.

One need but think of the difficulty experienced at the outset in endeavouring to avoid the adjacent strings in order to see how easy it is to get from one string to another, but directly we have got over our first difficulties, we find that that which we at first found difficult to avoid is by no means so easy of accomplishment as previously imagined when we endeavour to effect it.

If we practise the small strokes on the A string when the bow is close to the nut, we should be able to reach the E and D strings (for isolated notes) without any alteration in the height of the forearm and upper-arm. In the performance of quick passages this is a great advantage, as otherwise the weight of the whole arm being suddenly brought on to another string for a single note leads to scratching.

Having accomplished your short strokes successfully at the nut of the bow, endeavour to execute them when the forearm and hand form a straight line in the centre of the bow.

When we arrive at the point of the bow the same difficulties do not exist. We no longer have a direct downward pressure of the arm on the strings, and pressure has to be applied rather than taken off, so that if we desire to play quick passages at the point, the wrist will rise slightly as in the ordinary stroke whenever necessary, and no finger flexion should take place. If the forearm rises sufficiently to allow the stroke to be executed, and the same hold is maintained with the fingers, the wrist must rise of its own accord. On no account must the position of the hand in relation to the bow be changed.

At the point it is not possible to cross from one string to another without the arm being raised from the shoulder; therefore, if we desire to go from the G string to the

A or D there must be a corresponding drop in the height of the arm. Should we desire to cross over the strings near the nut of the bow using quite small strokes, practically only two positions of the arm are necessary—the two that are employed whilst playing on the A and D strings. Then, if we use a small rotary movement of the wrist, the two remaining strings may be reached without changing the height of the arm. When the middle of the bow is reached, only two strings can be played upon with any comfort (and these not too easily) without changing the height of the forearm. If we proceed to the point we find that it is almost impossible to play on more than one string with any comfort without changing the height of the right arm.

The rotary hand movement is of most use when applied to quick passages, as it is then that we find the chief difficulty in changing from one string to another by means of the whole arm movement. The quicker we play, the more difficult is it to move the whole arm in the space of time allowed, and consequently the more unsatisfactory the results.

I would recommend practising for a considerable time this finger flexion and wrist movement—together with the rotary movement of the hand for crossing over the strings—at the nut of the bow.

Almost any exercise in detached bowing can be employed for the purpose, but the two which I find of very great benefit are numbers 4 and 6 in Alard's Ten Etudes, Op. 10; numbers 2, 5 and 8 in Kreutzer and Casorti's Bogentechnik, whilst for more advanced players Dont's Etudes and Caprices (numbers 2 and 3), and Rode's Caprices are more suitable. Should any of the notes be found to be slurred it would be better to use a whole bow for the long notes, which will bring the detached ones alternatively at the point and nut, or to remove the slurs altogether.

Do not forget that should you endeavour to execute the wrist and finger flexion in the middle of the bow, it is necessary to employ a slight downward or upward forearm movement in conjunction with it, and that at the point no finger flexion at all is necessary, as the wrist executes the strokes without difficulty.

When you are crossing from one string to another, endeavour to maintain tensity, and during the process neither release pressure nor apply more than you had in the previous stroke.

To ensure that the tone is not broken the bow should be kept moving, and therefore directly it has completed its upward movement a downward motion immediately takes place without there being any break between the strokes. It should be possible to make the movement continuous.

In addition to this finger and wrist flexion being employed for all short notes, the movement, as already described, always forms the last portion of the upward stroke and the first of the downward. This, as previously stated, is so that the bows may be joined together, without there being any apparent break. Should stiffness be present it is impossible to execute the movement in the manner explained, whilst if too loose a hold is employed in all probability the bow will be dropped. This, however, is a better fault than retaining a vice-like grip on the stick. In either case there is a lack of control, but you are more likely to assume complete control of the bow if you are too loose than too stiff.

Remember that the knuckles should not be depressed, but in order to maintain the correct position of the hand towards the bow there is a gentle outward curve of the fingers of the right hand towards the stick. (*See illustration.*)

DIAGRAM VI.

Illustrating the gentle outward curve of the fingers. The latter should fall or lap over the bow in a gentle curve to the first joint (not beyond), with the exception of the fourth finger, the *tip* of which should actually rest on the top of the stick.

CHAPTER X.

32. LENGTH OF BOW IN RELATION TO DURATION OF NOTE.

It will now be apparent that long notes require long bows, and short notes short bows. For semiquavers and demisemiquavers (in quick time) only a delicate movement of the hand and fingers is necessary; for longer notes the wrist and forearm, until with minims and semibreves we find that the whole arm is employed. Though it is impossible to lay down any exact rules as to how much bow should be used for each note, this is the general principle.

To obtain a more perfect control of the bow, it is an excellent plan to move it over the strings about half an inch above them, without allowing it to come into contact with them. Much difficulty will be experienced in keeping the bow at the same height from the strings throughout the stroke, but if practised for a few minutes every day, the control will become much more perfect. It is *necessary* that one should obtain sufficient control to do this exercise without effort. I have previously explained that the bow does not merely rest on the strings with its own weight, but that it is at all times under the control of the player.

The actual amount of bow that is used for each note will largely depend upon the rapidity with which a passage is played. The character of the bowing must also be taken into consideration, as with staccato and spring bowing effects, only a small amount of the bow is used; but when we desire to obtain a perfect legato a large portion of the bow is moved over the strings.

33. LEGATO BOWING.

In the first instance, do not attach too much importance to the playing of what are termed "Fancy bowings," as they are acquired far more easily than legato bowings. In order to obtain a perfect legato it is necessary to practice for many years whilst even with the finest players their legato is constantly improving. Fancy bowings require nothing like the same amount of practice. As both the bow and strings are under a certain amount of tension, it is more natural for them to execute springing than legato effects.

That we may obtain control when crossing from one string to the other in the same bow (legato bowing), it is well to practise special studies. Alard's Ten Studies, Opus 10, Number 6, will be found particularly useful. It will be noticed that the bow crosses over two and sometimes three strings, and that a large number of notes has to be played in the same bow. Such passages are often found in the works of Brahms, and most players find considerable difficulty in playing them in anything approaching legato. As a matter of fact they are no more difficult than ordinary legato bowings if executed in the correct manner. Let me explain how this bowing should be accomplished.

The right arm moves down in one plane as though playing on one string, and when it is desired to go to a higher or lower string the hand merely makes a downward or upward movement, in order to bring the bow on to the string required. The movement of the hand is exactly the same as that previously explained when crossing over the strings with a small amount of bow for each note; the only difference being that now we are playing a number of such notes in each bow, and therefore we require the execution of a like number of hand movements.

Whenever possible, in the case of short bows, it is desirable to make movements from one string to another by means of the wrist (or rather the hand), especially in quick passages, as otherwise a sudden change of the position of the right arm leads to scratching and "digging."

34. GRADATIONS OF SOUND.

When playing piano passages the bow will move nearer the finger-board, and in forte passages closer to the bridge. Again, it will be found that when an open string is being sounded the bow will be further away from the bridge than when the string is considerably shortened by the fingers stopping notes in the higher positions.

Gradations of sound are also effected by the rate at which the bow is moving. If the bow is moved freely and quickly over the strings a full and round tone will be produced, but if it is pressed against the strings and moved slowly in a cramped manner the tone becomes tight. Therefore, endeavour to obtain a flowing bow which will produce a happy floating tone, as any stiffness only results in scratching—or at the best a sticky, tight tone.

In whatsoever position the bow rests upon the strings the hand retains the same relationship towards the stick, and at no time throughout the stroke should it change this relationship.

During the playing of piano passages the hold on the bow should not be relaxed, neither should it be tightened during forte passages. These are common faults.

PART III.

CHAPTER XI.

35. LEFT-HAND TECHNIQUE.

I SHALL now proceed to discuss the technique of the left hand. As previously explained, the violin is supported by means of the grip between the jaw or chin and the left shoulder, the neck of the violin being merely *placed* between the V formed by the thumb and the first finger.

36. THE THUMB.

I have already endeavoured to make it quite plain that the thumb does not grip the neck of the violin, but that it merely resists

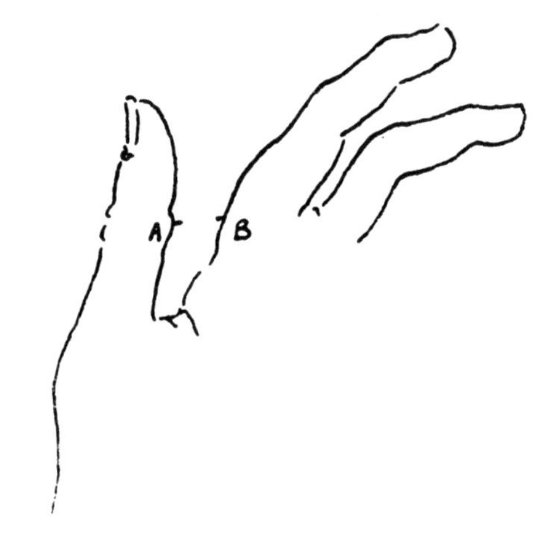

DIAGRAM VII.

Showing V in which neck of violin is placed. Contact should take place at A and B and not lower down the V.

Plate XI.

POSITION OF RIGHT HAND AND FINGERS AFTER FINGER FLEXION.

Explanation.

If this photograph is carefully compared with Plate X. it will be found that the upper-arm, elbow, and forearm remain in exactly the same position as previously, but that the hand has moved upwards (swung round slightly towards the player's face) and the little finger become curved, thereby enabling the last two or three inches of the bow to be used. The straightening of the fingers and lowering of the hand to the position illustrated in Plate X. forms the first portion of the downward stroke, and no movement of the forearm of upper-arm takes place until this has been completed. Note that the point of the bow, instead of moving round the back of the player, if anything moves slightly in the opposite direction.

Photograph by Wykeham.]

PLATE XI

the pressure of the fingers. On no account should the neck be allowed to slide down until it reaches the bottom of the V, as the soft flesh between the thumb and the first finger clings to the wood and makes sliding difficult.

I do not like to lay down any too hard and fast rules for the position of the left thumb, beyond the fact that its tip should not be too much above the level of the finger-board. If, however, the neck rests against the first joint of the thumb it will meet the case. In regard to whether it should be placed in front of, on a line with, or behind the first finger, I think that either of these positions may be adopted to suit individual players, the main point being that the thumb tip should be turned outwards and not inwards, as the latter leads to puckering of the loose skin on the thumb, which again interferes with sliding. Personally, I consider that in most cases it is preferable that the thumb should be slightly behind the forefinger, as it is then in a better position to slide underneath the neck when the hand slides to higher positions.

If in doubt as to the advisability of turning the thumb out in preference to curving it round the neck of the fiddle, try both ways and see which is the easier. You will find that when you curve your thumb it sticks, and makes your sliding far less sure and exact than if merely a small portion of it touches the neck. This statement can be easily verified by placing your thumb and forefinger round a broom handle. You will find that they do not slide so easily in encircling the stick as when only a small portion of each touches it, and it is almost unnecessary to mention that gripping prevents sliding altogether.

To ensure that your thumb does not grip the instrument it is an excellent plan to practise without the thumb, merely letting the fingers fall on the strings, meanwhile supporting the head of the violin on the chimney piece or anything of suitable height. The only difficulty in carrying out this sort of practice lies in the fact that most chimney pieces are not of sufficient height to ensure the violin being held in its correct position!

37. THE KNUCKLES AND HAND.

If you have your thumb in the normal position it will almost necessarily follow that the knuckles of the left hand are also correctly in position. The knuckles of the first finger will be slightly below the level of the finger-board; that of the second on a line with it, the third and fourth slightly higher.

The weakest part of the hand (towards the third and fourth fingers) will then be brought well above the strings, which counteracts in a large measure the feeling of feebleness otherwise apparent in the little finger.

When playing on the lower strings, that is the G and D, the hand will naturally be raised higher than when the notes occur on the E and A strings. Do not forget, therefore, that the position of the knuckles—and consequently the hand from the wrist—varies according to which string is being used. Whilst playing in the lower positions (viz., until the third is reached) the wrist, hand and forearm will form a straight line from the knuckles to the elbow. Once again let me emphasise that the left elbow should not rest against the body at any time during your practice, and until the third position is reached the hand should not touch the side of the violin.

(*Note.*—The movement of the left elbow has been previously described on page 40.)

CHAPTER XII.

38. FINGER ACTION.

WHETHER the fingers are actually on or off the strings, they should always be curved at the joints. Only the tips should be placed on the strings, and they should fall perpendicularly on the strings so as to effect a direct downward pressure.

Before you place your fingers on the strings remember the strings are moving (vibrating), and that it is therefore necessary for your fingers to exert a far greater pressure than does the bow. In addition, their action should be quite independent of the pressure of the bow on the strings.

After having stopped a note with any finger, lift it well above the strings so that each time it is brought into use it falls from

PLATE XII.

POSITION OF LEFT HAND AND FINGERS DURING PLAYING OF TENTHS.

(*See Chapter on Extensions.*)

The photograph illustrates the position of the fingers during the playing of a tenth, viz., from D in the third position to B in the first position.

Note the ease with which this is accomplished when played as directed. It has not even been necessary to straighten the fourth finger, which in this instance is only of ordinary length.

Photograph by Wykeham.]

PLATE XII

its greatest height and strikes the strings with considerable force.

Many amateurs never raise their fingers very far from the strings as they are frightened that in this case they may not strike the correct note when descending. The fingers, however, must fall from their greatest height with considerable velocity; on no account let them be sluggish in their movements. They should strike the strings in exactly the same manner as a hammer strikes a nail.

Let us begin by placing the first finger on the strings. Before doing so, observe that it is curved at both joints, then lifting its tip at least an inch from the strings allow it to strike the note without sounding it with the bow. If this is done with sufficient force the note should be distinctly audible each time the tip meets the strings. Practise this again and again, and having struck the same note each time, repeat the experiment with the remaining fingers. Should the finger alight on the note in the wrong position the first time, do not slither it up and down the strings until it is in the desired place, but lift it, and repeat the performance until successful. To do this correctly requires an effort of concentration, and the more you think of that which you are endeavouring to execute the more likely are you to accomplish it successfully.

Whilst the fingers remain on the strings the pressure at the tip is retained, but if a tight cramped position is adopted the player has a feeling of fatigue, and the finger consequently becomes lifeless. In order to avoid this, the fingers of the left hand should relax directly they leave the finger-board. If the fingers are straightened no relaxation takes place; but when they are bent and curved naturally above the finger-board it will be found that the tightness which was experienced while they remained on the strings disappears. (See plate 13.)

Unless relaxation takes place when the fingers are not actually stopping notes no finger technique can ever be obtained, as after a few minutes' playing they become weak, and for the time being almost cramped.

Flexibility is the result of relaxation which allows the fingers to recover after each movement.

It will be found that the fourth finger tires more easily than others, and that relaxation in this case is even more necessary. If you can educate yourself to relax your fingers you will obtain greater flexibility. On no account permit any stiffness to exist whilst the fingers are not doing work.

The following may help the pupil to understand this point a little more clearly :—

" If the muscles are not released by lifting the fingers and relaxing them at each joint they become cramped in their movement, and a feeling of weakness is soon apparent. They become temporarily muscle-bound, as athletes say. Every muscle in the body capable of being controlled by the will becomes affected in this way if a strained position is adopted for any length of time, so that it can be easily understood how necessary it is that all the fingers, especially the fourth, should be relaxed immediately they leave the strings. On no account should this take place during the playing of a note, as it will affect its physical and mental tensity. If there is no such relaxation the finger difficulty affects the mental powers, as, when the muscles become tired, the brain finds it too great an effort to make them carry out its ideas; and will power becomes affected through placing an unnatural strain on any part of the body."

Therefore it will be apparent that *lifting* the fingers is as important as hammering them on the strings.

In order to acquire technique without undue labour, it is necessary to know what your fingers are doing when not playing as much as when they are! Many players who find that their finger technique does not progress satisfactorily would see an immediate and rapid improvement if they paid a little attention to the correct method of lifting and relaxing their fingers whilst *not* on the strings. Sluggish movements of the fingers lead to sluggish technique, so ensure that your fingers are raised as high as possible from the strings without in any way affecting the position of the hand, and that they descend to their point of contact with great vigour.

When performing very rapid passages, it stands to reason that the fingers cannot be raised so far above the finger-board as in slower movements, but in this case they rest for such a short time on the strings that they have not time to become cramped. When, however, you practise quick passages, first play them very slowly for a number of times, lifting the fingers well above the strings between each note.

If you desire the third finger to descend on the strings, do not allow the remainder of the fingers to do the same thing. It only requires one finger to stop one note, and there is quite sufficient for all four fingers to do if they are employed at the correct time. You will find that they merely get in the way if set to work when there is nothing for them to do, besides which, as you never allow them to go to sleep, they are never really awake. Every finger must rest as long as it works, otherwise it will only go on strike. Clean technique will be the result of correct finger action; muddy technique means slovenly and untidy finger action.

At all costs avoid pressing the bow on the strings, because you are pressing with the fingers of the left hand. I cannot emphasise too strongly the fact that there should be complete independence of action between the left and right hands; they will work together only so long as they are independent. When not pressing sufficiently with the left hand matters will not be helped by placing more pressure on the bow. The reverse should be the case, the finger tips *always* pressing more firmly on the strings than the bow.

I wish to make it quite clear that at no time should the fingers of the left hand become "stiff" or "cramped" any more than those of the right. There is a decidedly firm downward pressure during the stopping of each note in order to maintain tensity, but this is merely a firmly controlled flexibility (which makes vibrato possible) and does not necessitate great muscular strain or effort.

I advise my pupils to devote a certain amount of time each day to the following method of developing flexibility of left-hand technique, which for want of a better name I have called "silent practice," as it is without the use of the bow.

It is extremely simple and merely consists of raising the fingers in a curve from the knuckles as high as possible above the strings and allowing them to strike the strings with considerable force. *Each note as it is struck should be distinctly audible to the player.* In the event of there being any stiffness the notes will not be heard. The fingers should fall direct from their greatest height to the point of contact with considerable velocity, and the finger action should not be prepared by a half-way movement towards the strings. In this manner the correct action of the fingers *from the knuckles* is developed.

Almost every imaginable passage can be practised in this way.

CHAPTER XIII.

39. THE THIRD POSITION.

After the first position, the third is considered to be more easily acquired than any other on the violin. This is on account of the fact that the hand is allowed to rest against the side of the instrument. The whole hand will be conveyed by means of the forearm from the first to the third position, when the base of the hand touches the violin. The forearm will move from the elbow joint, and the position of the wrist should not in any way be changed. The V formed between the forearm and upper-arm merely shortens its angle. For all positions from the third upwards, the hand remains touching the instrument, but for the higher positions the thumb gradually slides underneath the neck and the hand consequently more above the finger-board, until the desired position is reached.

40. THE SECOND POSITION.

The second position is generally considered to be one of the most difficult, on account of the fact that there is nothing to tell one when one is there; and for this reason the third position is usually studied first. At the same time I cannot emphasise too strongly the importance of studying the second position as carefully as the third, for there are many passages that can only be played by its use. In this position the hand should not touch the violin.

41. HIGHER POSITIONS.

I have dealt with the first and third positions only, as when the player has progressed thus far he should be in a position to undertake the study of the remaining positions without considerable difficulty. I would, however, emphasise very strongly one point; that is, that each and every position should be studied assiduously until it is mastered, and the player does not have to hesitate in order to think which finger should be used for a certain note or in which position he is playing. As each higher position is approached the hand, and consequently the fingers, move slightly round the violin and above the finger-board.

CHAPTER XIV.

SLIDING.

42. DEFINITION.

BEFORE explaining in what manner the slide should be executed, I should like to quote the following from Grove's Dictionary of Music :—

"To violinists the 'slide' is one of the principal vehicles of expression; at the same time affording a means of passing from one note to another at a distance. The rules governing the 'slide' are not restricted, as its use and effect entirely depend upon the judgment of the player, but the following directions are generally observed: A 'slide' is effected by allowing the finger already upon the string to move up and down to within a fourth or third of the new note. Care should be taken to keep the fingers strictly within the range of each new position.

"Another kind of 'slide' is made by moving the finger over two or more adjoining semitones without interruption.

"An imitation of the matchless legato which the human voice alone can attain, violinists frequently employ a 'slide' limited to adjoining notes. The third 'slide' is entirely of a brilliant type and belongs to the virtuoso *par excellence*, having originated with Paganini. It consists in executing chromatic passages, singly or in thirds, octaves or other combinations, entirely with the same fingers. This 'slide' did not come into general use until the end of the eighteenth century or the beginning of the nineteenth; yet its sister acquirements, the tremolo and shift, were known to violinists a century earlier."

There is one passage in the above quotation to which I would particularly draw the reader's attention, viz.: "Its use and effect entirely depend upon the judgment of the player." Herein lies the secret of most sliding. It depends on the judgment and ability of the player! As a result we find that sliding is perhaps more abused than anything else in a violinists' equipment. Most Bohemian types of violinists consider that no note should be played without a preparatory slide, and in consequence their playing degenerates into a sort of caterwauling which can only appeal to the mentally unstrung.

Nearly all wind instruments, and also the piano and organ, are incapable of sliding, yet the results obtained have not been considered unsatisfactory, and it is impossible for me to state too emphatically that unless the slide is employed by an artist, or by an individual possessing taste and a sensitive nature, it is almost better left out! Used in the correct manner and with sufficient judgment it is a most effective addition to a violinist's outfit, and no string player can be considered to be even passably efficient unless he is able to execute it in a satisfactory manner. If, however, it is employed upon any and every occasion, the result will only give pleasure to those who have not music in their souls.

The passage from "Grove's" above quoted admirably states the position in regard to sliding, and also places the slides in their correct order. I shall endeavour to explain them as enumerated.

43. SLIDES EMPLOYING TWO FINGERS TO A HIGHER POSITION.

The first slide is effected by allowing the finger already on the strings to move up or down to within a fourth or third of the new note. To this I would add that it may move to within a second of the note to be played.

Without doubt the slide is one of the principal mediums of expression on the violin, but if this first slide is executed in the correct manner it should hardly be audible as a slide and rather gives the effect of striking a note from or to a great height.

Let us take an instance. We desire to slide from B with the first finger on the A string to B in the fifth position on the same string. The first finger moves from B to F or F sharp (whichever note happens to be in the key), and the fourth finger is then brought down upon the strings. The whole slide must be executed as one movement, and there should be no appreciable break between the movement of the first finger and the arrival of the fourth at its appointed position. Supposing we desire to slide from the first position to the fifth, and that the first note is to be played with the first finger and the following one with the second; the first finger will slide to the fifth position direct when the second finger is placed on the strings.

Presuming we desire to slide from G on the E string to D in the fourth position. The second finger slides to C or C sharp, as the case may be, and at the moment of arrival in the new position the third finger drops on the strings.

Again, we are playing G with the third

finger on the D string, and we wish to play E in the fifth position. The third finger slides to D when the fourth finger strikes the desired note.

In these slides it will be noticed that there is an auxiliary note preparatory to the note to be played. It is an excellent plan, when beginning to practise the slide, to actually play this note, afterwards, of course, leaving it out altogether.

It is important to remember during sliding that the thumb should not grip the neck of the violin. The less pressure the easier will it be to move from one position to the next.

44. SLIDES EMPLOYING TWO FINGERS TO A LOWER POSITION.

So far, I have dealt with upward slides, now let me give you a few instances which will explain how downward slides should be executed. We have the fourth finger in the fifth position on the G string, and we desire to slide to the octave below. The fourth finger will slide back from A to D when it is immediately removed, the first finger having previously been placed on the lower A. Again, we are playing E in the fifth position on the E string, and we desire to play G in the first position. The third finger will be drawn back until the hand is now in the first position and then removed, the second finger having first been placed in position on G.

45. FAULTY SLIDING.

It will be seen that the finger already on the strings actually makes the slide, and that the one which is about to play the note required is not brought into action until the desired position is reached, when it falls directly upon the note to be played. In order to make this point quite clear, I will give an instance as to how *not* to execute the slide. If you have the second finger on the A string in the first position, and you wish to play B with the fourth finger in the fifth position, do not place the fourth finger on E and then slide to B; the result will, in all probability, be anything but satisfactory, and you will find the fourth finger either does not go sufficiently far or travels just a little beyond the note you desire to play. In addition, when slides are executed in this manner an unpleasant "scoop" is usually noticeable. I think that the single instance given will be sufficient to make my meaning quite clear, and no further illustrations should be necessary. Provided that the slide is played in the correct manner, it leaves the impression that the note has been hit, whereas in the other instance the reverse is the case.

46. SLIDES EMPLOYING ONE FINGER.

Now I shall deal with the second slide, viz., when the *same* finger slides over two or more notes on the same string. In order to ensure that no scoop is apparent in this slide, it is essential that it should be executed without pressure. There must be no hesitation, and the hand should move quickly from the first to the second note without interruption. Many violinists who are not altogether of the "first water" affect this slide in almost everything they do. They imagine that ordinary notes not preceded by a slide are ineffective, so before they have hardly reached one note they are slithering away on to the next. I need hardly say that both taste and judgment are sadly at fault in such instances. This slide should rarely be employed and then, as previously stated, it must be perfectly executed. If used by an artist, it is in safe hands, but a most dangerous weapon in the hands of others.

47. SLIDES TO ADJACENT NOTES WITH THE SAME FINGER OR FINGERS.

The third slide, which consists of playing a number of tones or semitones singly or in thirds, sixths, octaves or tenths, etc., with the same finger, only applies to the advanced player, and to him it is not more than ordinarily difficult. In any case, it is accomplished far more easily than would be the case if the notes had to be played with different fingers. It is usually executed from a higher to a lower position, and more often than not in semitones. A vibrato or exaggerated tremolo is begun by means of the left hand, and the fingers are then dragged downwards over the strings. It is of little use my endeavouring to explain this to the beginner but the more advanced player learns it very easily. I would, however, just mention that in bringing the hand downwards the wrist is turned outwards, so that it is nearer to the scroll of the violin than is any other portion of the hand or arm.

48. SLIDES EMPLOYED IN SCALE PASSAGES.

In the practice of scales (and all scale passages) we come across another slide not previously described. For instance, we are playing the scale of G major in three octaves; we desire to play the last octave and our finger rests on G on the E string in the first position. The next note in the scale is

A. If, however, we apply Rule 1 in sliding, let us consider what the result will be. The second finger will go to B, when it will be removed from the string, the first finger having been previously placed on A. This method of sliding cannot, therefore, be considered satisfactory. In our previous rule we noticed that when sliding to a higher position the auxiliary note was always lower than the one actually to be played, and when sliding back to a lower position, the auxiliary note was above the one we were about to strike. In this instance, however, we are proceeding to play a note in a higher position, and the auxiliary note is above the one to be played. Therefore, if the slide is executed in the manner first described, we shall never be able to play scale passages without intermediate notes being apparent.

One of the chief difficulties in playing scale passages in pure legato is to get them sufficiently smooth so that the slides are inaudible. In order to effect this and any other slides of a similar nature, we have to prepare the slide in a different way. Directly, therefore, that we start moving the hand from the first to the third position, we place the finger below the one we are using on the strings, and the second finger is removed when it has travelled only one note.

By the time that the second finger is removed from the strings, the first finger will have taken up its position in practically the same spot (as the hand is moving all the time) and have completed the slide to the third position, and so on.

In order to make this more clear, let me explain the method of procedure once again. We are going from G on the E string in the first position to A on the same string in the third position. The second finger begins moving from G to A; the first finger is then placed on the strings, and the second finger being removed, the first takes its place. Therefore, when notes are adjacent to each other and a higher finger is on the strings than that required in order to play the next note, the slide is begun by the finger already on the strings, and completed by the finger below it.

49. IN WHICH BOW THE SLIDE SHOULD TAKE PLACE.

As in everything else in connection with violin playing, bowing plays a very important part in the slide. It is, therefore, essential that the player is aware in which bow the slide takes place. The following is a fairly safe rule to go upon. Slides should take place at the termination of a note (with extremely rare exceptions) so that the change of note synchronises with the change of bow. The slide is completed in the old bow, and does not take place at the commencement of a fresh stroke. In this manner each note is attacked cleanly, and not during the performance of a slide. It will be understood that one can take away from the end of a note, but not from the beginning.

In order to make this a little more clear, let me endeavour to explain further. Should the note before a slide be played by a down-bow, and the following note be an up-bow in a different position, then the slide will take place at the conclusion of the down-bow, and not at the commencement of the new (up) bow. The same will apply when the note before the change of position is played with an up-bow, and the subsequent note in a different position in a down-bow. In this case the slide will be made at the conclusion (the very last moment) of the up-bow, so that the down-bow begins on a fresh note. In other words, the hand should always be in the new position at the beginning of a new stroke, and not after the stroke has begun.

50. MENTAL CALCULATION OF SLIDES.

The distance of any slide is calculated mentally, and it will be found that each slide can be learned more quickly by closing the eyes during practice. Make the slide without the aid of the bow, listening each time for the fall of the finger on the strings, then test it with a short stroke at the point.

When you close your eyes they are not talking to your brain of all the interesting things within their vision, so that your brain is able to concentrate more easily on the matter in hand.

It is of no assistance to see the distance of a slide, you must *feel* it.

CHAPTER XV.

51. FINGERING.

Scales and Arpeggi.

One of the most important points to be remembered in connection with left-hand technique is that there should be uniformity in fingering. If similar passages are always fingered in the same manner it does away with much of the complexity which otherwise makes the technique rather involved. In addition, it is only possible to play some passages when they are fingered in a certain manner. There is such a vast difference between good and bad fingering and the subject is such a lengthy one that it is hardly possible to deal with it in one chapter. So I propose merely treating the fingering of scales, in order that this may serve as an example. Let us deal with scales in two octaves to begin with. G, A and B being in the first position require no special fingering, but if we commence all the scales above them in two octaves with the second finger on the G string the hand remains in one position throughout, and all the tones and semitones occur in exactly the same place. Therefore the scale of C will be played in the second position; D in the third; E in the fourth, and so on. If we begin the scales in three octaves in like manner, making all the slides on the E string, this greatly facilitates progress and simplifies our work.

The fingering for the chromatic scale can be found in almost any reliable text book. The one point which I desire to impress upon my readers is that there should be as much uniformity in their fingering as it is possible to attain. When we finger our scales, arpeggi and double notes on some definite plan, we have at least a big ground work upon which to build.

The only general remark I should like

to make which is applicable to all fingerings is: Changes of fingering should take place wherever possible on the beat and not on unaccented notes. In this way the rhythm of the music is assisted, otherwise it is disturbed.

Whilst on the subject of scales and arpeggi I cannot emphasise too strongly their importance. They form the groundwork of all technique, and help to gain facility more than any other form of practice. As much time as possible should be given to their daily study. I do not wish it to be thought that I am recommending this in connection with children's study whilst they are at school. As a matter of fact, the less a child is bothered with technique the more likely will it be that he or she will retain a love of music. In the place of hours of study of technique for children, I would advocate plenty of opportunities of listening to good music, lectures about musicians, on musical instruments, combined with plenty of class singing. Folk songs should be taught to children as they are the songs of the people, and are peculiarly applicable to children on account of their pure, unaffected sentiment. The less children have to do with technique the better, and in any case the time so spent during the early years of their lives will in all probability be thrown away. My remarks on scale practice apply to older players who are intent on acquiring technical facility.

52. HOW TO PRACTISE.

Many pupils throw away hours of their time in needless labour which might be more profitably spent did they but know how to utilise the time at their disposal. For instance, we have a study to prepare. The usual method is to begin at the beginning and carry on, regardless of mistakes, to the conclusion. We then begin again and perpetrate the same fiasco once more; repeating it until the time at our disposal has gone by.

The benefits derived from such practice are slight, and in many cases the time thus spent is not conducive to progress of any description. I think the following will be found a more satisfactory method of procedure:—

Let us begin once again at the beginning; this time we stumble after having executed only a few notes. Directly the mistake is discovered it is rectified; but it is not sufficient to rectify it once, we must be certain that we shall not make the same mistake again, so we repeat that particular passage or group of notes (it may only be two or three) until we are certain that it presents no difficulty; then we proceed on our own way until we come across another difficulty and deal with it in like manner.

We have now discovered two of our stumbling blocks and have dealt with them by themselves, having mastered each separately. This at least is progress; but now let us see if we can master both difficulties in succession. In all probability it will be found that we stumble once again over either one or the other; therefore, we keep on returning to the same spot, and having conquered our two difficulties in succession, we proceed to a third, taking it not in conjunction with the first two, but by itself. When this also is mastered we return to our second difficulty, and see if we can play the passage containing both; and this being accomplished, to our first, in order to discover if it is possible to link up the whole passage without faults.

When this method is adopted we shall have mastered a certain number of difficulties during our first hour's practice, and then when we next begin to study, having practised the first portion of our exercise we do not go over it again as we have fresh fields in which to work, so we begin where we left off at the previous practice.

In this manner our difficulties become apparent during our early practice; they are mastered as they arise, and instead of stumbling over the exercises with little or no intelligence until we have got tired of them, we take a delight in surmounting our successive difficulties and placing our structure together until the whole building is complete.

Do let me take this opportunity of warning players against the malady of wasting their time in fruitless and altogether inane study. It often occurs with amateurs that they hate being stopped. This is a sure sign that they are not particularly sensitive to their own shortcomings, and that they prefer to continue along the wrong path rather than be guided in the straight and narrow way!

I know many amateurs who meet regularly for the study (so-called) of chamber music, but I have actually heard them say before they begin: "Now whatever happens, for goodness' sake don't let us stop." Before the first movement is half way through the viola has lost his place (somehow or other he is usually the first, one does not know why) and is making unhappy attempts at the expense of the remainder of the players in order to find it. Ere long his efforts succeed in putting out the second violin; and he, too, endeavours to fall in in the correct place; then our friend the 'cellist is placed out of action, and finally the first violinist is compelled to retire from the unequal combat! I have seen this sort of thing happen again and again, and the players have thought that they were practising! How silly and futile it has all been; nobody has gained any particular benefit, for when the last instrumentalist lost his place they merely went back to the beginning and charged through the work again! They have gained little or no experience, and have only succeeded in wasting much time in order to murder the composer's work. Had they stopped when the viola lost his place and discovered the difficulty in the first instance, they would more probably have been able to complete the work satisfactorily, when they could have begun at the beginning and played it with increased intelligence.

This instance will serve to show how vital it is that every moment of one's time should be spent in careful study, instead of wasting in a fruitless manner the valuable moments at one's disposal.

The world scoffs at what are termed "pains-taking efforts" when these are offered to an audience by an artist who is supposed to have completed his study; but when we practise, it is our capacity for being able to take pains that leads in the end to our being able to give that air of careless ease to technique which is so necessary. In the finished article, our efforts to play the violin must *appear* at least effortless, but until we are quite sure of our ground and have undertaken the preliminary study necessary to the development of the desirable effect termed "ease," we must indeed go slowly.

53. DOUBLE STOPPING.

Double stopping should be practised directly one is able to place the first finger on the strings. It is an unfortunate fact that this department is often left until one has studied the instrument for a number of years, the result being that the player finds it difficult to acquire any degree of proficiency in playing double notes. The reason for this is easy to perceive. He has never placed his fingers really cleanly on the strings so as to miss the adjacent ones. If, however, we begin by placing our first finger on F natural on the E string in the first position and then test it against the open A string, we have our first lesson in playing double notes. Again, when we get the second finger on the strings we can try it in conjunction with the string above, thus making a third. The first finger when playing on the G, D and A strings can be tested against the string above in like manner, making a fourth, and the third finger played with the string below makes an octave. Therefore, as we progress with single notes, we are developing double stopping, and not leaving it to be crowded into our equipment at the last moment. Later, when we arrive at the second position, we adopt the same policy and try the notes in the first instance against open strings, which enables us to test their purity.

Having accomplished so much against the open strings, we have commenced to build the foundations of our structure in the correct manner. As we have made a strong foundation we are now enabled to build upon it without fear that the whole will come tumbling about our ears.

So far we have only placed one finger on the strings which has been tried against an open note, but now we begin to bring a second finger into use. We have placed our first finger on F, B or E in the first position, and tested each against the open strings. Having assured ourselves that they are pure, we place the third finger on the lower string, making a third. This we lift again and again until we find it always possible to drop it on the correct note. So much accomplished, we do the same with our second finger, leaving the first and third down. Then we reverse the process, placing the second finger on the strings, and trying the third on either the string above or below, making a sixth or a fourth. Having succeeded to our satisfaction, we try the fourth on the string below, making again a third. These simple exercises in the first position can be practised in numberless combinations, and they lead to the overcoming of that terrible fear of double stopping which lurks in almost every amateur's mind. Double stopping must go hand in hand with single notes from the outset, and on no account should it be left until the player has attained a passably satisfactory technique, for it leads in the first instance to his placing the tips of his fingers on the strings in the correct manner, whereas if left until later it will be found that the fingers have never really descended cleanly on the notes but have always touched adjacent strings.

PART IV.

CHAPTER XVI.

BOWING.

54. SAUTILLE MODERE—HEAVY OR MODERATE SAUTILLE.

I SHALL now endeavour to explain the various fancy bowings which, if correctly executed, can be employed so effectively by the player. The first of these is Sautillé Modéré (moderate Sautillé). Moderate Sautillé bowing must not be confused with ordinary Sautillé, which is of a lighter nature; the former is a heavy detached stroke, the latter a spring bowing. Moderate Sautillé should be played from the nut of the bow, using about a third or fourth of its length. It is executed by means of the wrist and fingers as previously described for short bows, in conjunction with a slight movement of the forearm. The bow is brought into contact with the strings whilst moving, and lifted from them at the conclusion of each stroke. Begin the stroke fairly close to the nut, with the bow about an inch above the strings. As the bow comes into contact with the strings it should be moving either upwards or downwards. If this is not observed, scratching will be the net result.

To begin with, the wrist and fingers will be well curved, and directly the bow touches the strings the fingers are quickly straightened whilst the wrist is lowered. In the upward stroke this is merely reversed.

It is important to remember three points in connection with this bowing :—

1. That the bow is moving *before* it touches the strings.

2. That the speed with which the bow is moving affects the accent more considerably than the force with which the hair strikes the strings.

3. That the force with which the hair strikes the strings is actually very slight, and that the accent is given to the note by means of the forefinger pressing firmly against the stick.

Endeavour to get away from the idea that the bow at any time works *into* the strings. The violin is such a delicate instrument that it does not require the application of physical strength in order to get the best results. It is necessary that there should be great physical and mental control, however.

In every bowing that you endeavour to execute always impress upon yourself the necessity of moving the bow *across* the strings rather than *into* them. In the case of accented bowings, as in the present instance, any accent that is given the note at its beginning should be immediately released directly the note is played. Pressure applied in order to give this accent should be released in the fraction of a second, and if the bow strikes the strings with too much force it is impossible to control the spring that will result. In addition, the strings will not be able to vibrate uniformly, having received a shock from which it takes a certain amount of time to recover. I would recommend Alard's Violin School, Part II., in which an excellent study occurs for the development of this bowing.

55. LE GRAND DETACHE.

This bowing produces a slightly similar, though not such a heavy effect, the chief differences being that it is executed towards the point of the bow (not in the middle), that it has to be played quicker, and the accent at the commencement of each note is not so apparent, on account of the fact that the bow remains on the strings throughout. The downward stroke is dragged (or drawn), and the upward pushed. As we are playing at the point of the bow no finger flexion is necessary, the forearm and wrist completing the movement. In order that the bowing may be executed satisfactorily, it is necessary to practise moving the bow quite quickly during the stroke.

Let us place the bow on the strings about a third of its distance from the point, and then without applying pressure, commence to move it quickly towards the tip of the bow. During the stroke we have given a slight accent to the note, swelling it out as it were, by means of the forefinger, and in order to get the effect of brilliance at the beginning of the stroke, the bow has been drawn very quickly—with a tug, as it were. Half way through the stroke the velocity of the movement *decreases*, and with it the pressure of the forefinger. We immediately commence the next stroke without there being any apparent break between each note. We then obtain an undulating result, which is a sort of cross between legato and staccato; the notes are, as it were, linked up or connected, and yet at the same time we obtain the effect of their being detached. Exercises for the study of this bowing may be found in the second part of Alard's Violin School already mentioned, but almost any exercise in detached bowing will serve equally well.

56. MARTELE BOWING.

This is also executed at the point, and if the previous bowing—le grand détaché—has been mastered, it should present no difficulties, as there is only one essential difference between them. With "le grand détaché" the accent should not be executed at the beginning of the note—martélé bowing has a decided accent at the commencement of each note. In martélé there is no undulating effect, but each note is played quickly and decidedly, when the bow comes to rest on the strings. The accent at the beginning of the note is given by means of the forefinger, but the pressure should be released directly the stroke is taken. There is a very decided pause between the completion of one note and the commencement of the next. Thus the bow remains stationary for a certain period, according to the length of the note played. As the stroke is taken the forefinger presses against the stick, but the pressure is released directly the bow is drawn downwards or upwards.

The effect is rather "stilted," and the bowing is employed wherever a sharp accent is necessary. Do not allow the wrist or arm to become stiff during the movement, or to exert too much pressure either at the commencement or during the stroke. The bowing should be executed by means of the forearm and wrist, and without finger flexion.

CHAPTER XVII.

57. SAUTILLE.

Of the many fancy bowings in the repertory of a violinist, sautillé and staccato are found to be the most difficult. Numerous times have I been told by pupils that they find it impossible to execute these two bowings whenever they desire to do so, and that sometimes sautillé or staccato simply will not come! Even with far more advanced players I have found that they have to "get going," as it were, before they can accomplish them. Some days they find that they can do them, and other days not! If we consider for a moment, this is absurd, and only leads to one conclusion—that the methods employed when the bowings are correctly played are different to those used on other occasions. If it is possible to make the bow spring on Tuesday there is no particular reason why it should not be made to do so on Wednesday. The weather does not affect such things, and it is the player who is at fault. Therefore, it will be seen that if the same methods are always employed, the same results will accrue. Herein lies the crux of the situation. One day we do one thing, and the next another. If we always do the same thing we shall produce the same results.

Firstly, what is the result that should be obtained? We should look for a series of gentle springs either in one or separate bows. The springs must be of equal height and duration.

The bowing is effected by *utilising the natural spring of the stick* when the hair is dropped from a slight height (*at about the middle of the bow) upon the strings. If this fact is realised, the rest is easy. The player

* *Note.*—The middle of the bow is at the point of balance and not half-way between the nut and the point.

does *not* make the bow bounce—it is natural for it to do so, and it is in the utilisation of this natural spring that success lies. The bowing, however, is one of extreme delicacy, and there is such a slight perceptible difference between the correct and the incorrect manner of doing it, that it is essential the player should be under the observation of his teacher at the first attempt. Nearly all players, by endeavouring to make the bow bounce, defeat their own end by interfering with the natural spring of the bow, as the assistance actually required is almost infinitesimal.

The springs must be of equal height, therefore the length of bow employed must in each case be the same. It also applies that the wrist movement and finger flexion must never vary.

In the downward stroke the hand works a little more downwards than usual, and in the up stroke, a little more upwards. For instance, if we execute sautillé bowing in single notes on the A string: in the downward stroke, the hand will incline the stick slightly more towards the E, and in the upward stroke towards the D.

I think I previously mentioned that all spring bowings, together with staccato, are executed by the bow working in two planes, and that legato is effected by the whole arm and hand moving in one plane. It will now be seen that I intended to convey in this particular bowing the hand has an independent action slightly out of the plane in which the arm is moving. This action causes the bow pressure to be unequal during the stroke. At the beginning, as the bow drops on the strings, it is pressed slightly into them, but being held with such a delicate control, it is not pressed firmly against them. The effect of this movement will be understood. When the hand works slightly downwards it has moved out of the plane in which the rest of the arm is moving, therefore it causes a slight rebound on the part of the bow. To do this, however, the latter must be travelling with a certain amount of speed, otherwise no particular result will accrue.

We have therefore played our note, and the bow has rebounded perhaps the eighth of an inch (certainly not more) from the strings. At this point we catch it, as it were, and then repeat exactly the same process in the upward bow.

In practising this slowly, it is an excellent plan to work in the manner just described, catching the bow each time it rebounds; but in the actual performance of spring bowings the movement is far too rapid to catch the bow in the upward and downward stroke. Indeed, it is not necessary that we should do so, for, as I have previously explained, the bow bounces of its own accord.

Having decided what we are about to attempt, let us now practise in a slightly different manner. Place the bow on the strings at its point of balance (which is slighly below the middle) and move it up and down in exactly the same way that you would do for legato bows, employing the wrist movement and finger flexion as previously described. Now if you gradually accelerate the speed of the movement and at the same time move your hand slightly (but ever so slightly) downwards in the down and upwards in the up strokes, you will find that the bow begins to spring quite naturally. It will need a considerable amount of application, and in the first instance a great deal of patience in order to bring this about, but having once acquired the sensitive touch necessary to its performance, you will find no difficulty in executing the same bowing on subsequent occasions, provided that you employ the same means.

Do not, on any account, endeavour to lift the bow from the strings at the conclusion of each note. To begin with, however, in order to get a slight accent on the first note, it *is* necessary to raise it about an eighth of an inch above the strings, and let the bow fall as you take your first stroke. Subsequently no such action on your part is necessary. It will be seen that had you not dropped the bow upon the strings the first note—and possibly the second—would have been in legato, as the bow could not have begun springing without the initial impulse.

Further, when practising this bowing, do not drop the bow on the strings until you have mastered the stroke by beginning from legato. Should you raise the bow too much from the strings in the first instance there will be a resultant spring, which it is impossible to control, so that it is only necessary to raise the hair very slightly above the strings before taking the first stroke.

I would emphasise that legato bowing is the basis of all others, and that only the slightest variation is necessary in order to create altogether different effects. Let me mention once again that if you have the correct movement it follows that the bowing will also be correct, and that if you can do it one day and not another it is simply because you employ different methods on different occasions.

Should any stiffness be apparent in the movement of the hand and fingers, it will be impossible for you to execute sautillé bowings. I know of no better exercises on bowing than those contained in the second part of Alard's Violin School, and the same remark applies to all the subsequent bowings.

These observations apply to sautillé bowings executed on one string, and when you have mastered them in this way there still remain some difficulties to be got over, for you will find that when it is desired to cross from one string to another the bow, for some unaccountable reason, suddenly stops springing! If, however, it is remembered to turn the hand slightly more downwards when going to a higher string, and a little more upwards when going to a lower string, we shall discover that with a short amount of practice it is possible to cross from one string to another, without stopping the spring of the bow. In this connection it may be necessary to slightly change the height of the upper-arm, but *the whole weight must be kept entirely from the strings*, and any movement made by the arm should be executed between strokes and not during the playing of the notes.

There is one other point which I find of

the greatest assistance in crossing over the strings, and if it is recollected there will be far less difficulty with string bowings than would otherwise be the case. Remember at all times that it is the manner in which the note is played before crossing over the strings that makes or mars the subsequent note. In other words, the hand must be *prepared* in order to get it in the required position in sufficient time to execute the following bow. If anything, there should be a slightly larger finger flexion and hand movement *before* crossing over, as in this manner we make sure that we do not stiffen during the playing of the following note.

58. SAUTILLE ARPEGGI BOWINGS.

In the previous chapter I have dealt with sautillé bowings on the same string, and I shall now endeavour to explain how they should be executed when crossing over three or four strings in the same bow. Really there is very little to be said on this point, as I have already outlined the principle of all spring bowings. Once again the hand works slightly more downwards in the down bow, and a little more upwards during the up bow. The chief difference, however, lies in the fact that we are now playing over three or four strings, each one of which is at a different angle to the bow. In addition, it is not possible to reach all the strings without lowering and raising the forearm and upper-arm. If, however, we use slightly more bow than in sautillé bowings on one string, in conjunction with a downward movement of the upper-arm, and a backward movement of the elbow reversing this in the up bow, we shall be able to reach all the strings without difficulty. Sautillé arpeggio bowings are executed by working the arm and bow in slightly different planes. The forearm moves downwards and upwards as though crossing over the strings as in legato bowings, but in the result the bow is caused to spring on account of the fact that the upper-arm is moving across the strings or slightly *into* them, as it were.

Let us try this bowing, and see how the

principle works. In the first place the bow is about an eighth of an inch above the G string (slightly below its middle), and as it moves towards the E string, the whole arm from the elbow will move slightly downwards, the hand being inclined a little more towards the strings than is ordinarily the case. If the correct amount of bow is used and no pressure applied we shall observe a slight spring as the bow touches each string. When we arrive at the E string, we catch it as it rebounds from this, and giving the upward stroke a slight impetus, repeat the process in the reverse until the G string is reached.

It is important to observe in the case of sautillé arpeggio bowings that the wrist is quite flexible during the down and up bows, and that it plays a very important part by moving freely during their execution. The fingers should also retain a sensitive control, just maintaining the *balance* of the stick, so as not to interfere with its spring.

Do not endeavour to play this bowing simply by holding the stick between the forefinger and thumb, and merely "waggling" the wrist in an uncontrolled manner, as the effect will not be satisfactory. It will be found that unless the bow is controlled by the player the hair will slither along the strings more often than spring from one to another. The control of the stick should at all times be tensely sensitive. By tensely, I do not mean stiffly. Stiffness destroys control; tensity helps it.

In the first instance, practise the bowings in the downward stroke, catching the bow each time it rebounds from the E string. Having mastered this, repeat the same movement inversely in the upward stroke. As the bow touches the strings in each instance the angle of the hand and arm should be immediately altered, so that the hair rebounds on to the next string at a different angle.

Once again, let me emphasise the fact that the downward and upward strokes should be exactly the same, for if more bow is used in one than the other the spring will at once be arrested.

When the bowing is executed nearer the

nut a larger spring will be effected than when towards the point, consequently a larger amount of bow must be used, and this remark also applies to sautillé bowings on one string.

It will be seen, then, that we are able to vary the tempi of the bowing as we desire, without in any way interfering with its effectiveness; for if the spring is higher the bow is consequently above the strings for a longer period than when only a slight spring is effected. Perhaps I should explain that it is impossible to practise this bowing very slowly, as directly the bow touches the strings it should bounce on to the next, and the next, and so on. Therefore the arm should be lowered immediately the bow touches the strings in the down and raised in the up strokes.

CHAPTER XVIII.

59. RICOCHET OR ELASTIC STACCATO.

THERE is still one other effect that can be obtained by means of what is practically a sautillé bowing, but which is usually known as Ricochet. It is accomplished by dropping the bow on the strings and allowing it to rebound on one or a number of occasions in the same bow.

In Paganini's "Caprices" many instances of this bowing occur. One of the chief difficulties, however, in connection with playing a large number of notes on one or more strings in the same bow lies in the fact that the spring varies according to the position of the bow on the strings. If, however, the bow is dropped on the strings for the first note, and the first finger kept gently pressing against the stick with the hand inclined slightly towards it, it will be found that when the bow is drawn downwards or upwards it continues to spring of its own accord. Avoid at all times a digging or scratching tone; real notes should be the result obtained if ricochet bowings are executed in the correct manner. This bowing can be executed in either the down or the up stroke towards the upper half of the bow.

60 SPRINGING OR FLYING STACCATO.

This bowing has a similar effect to a light staccato and is more easily executed than solid staccato.

The first finger should be pressed firmly against the stick, and the hand inclined well towards the bow. If the bow is then moved upwards in conjunction with a nervous motion of the wrist the springing will continue during the playing of a number of notes. Begin with the bow *on* the strings near the point, and push the first note, using plenty of bow, at the same time allowing the wrist to rise. One of the chief points to be observed is that the wrist rises, if anything, more than is usually the case in ordinary legato bowings—which remark applies to solid staccato. It will also be found that the bow springs at a different rate in different parts of its length, and unless kept towards the middle the bow will get out of control.

In all staccato bowings it is important to remember that the less bow used the better is the effect. If we use too much bow, staccato becomes legato.

Before endeavouring to play any passages with this bowing, the notes should be learned from memory, as the fingers of the left hand have to be fitted in according to the rate at which the bow is springing.

I have purposely treated this bowing briefly as it is difficult to describe the exact effect except by illustration.

61. STACCATO.

Perhaps of all the bowings that a violinist endeavours to execute, what is known as ordinary, solid staccato is found to be the most difficult. There is no reason whatsoever why this should be the case, as the bowing is by no means the monopoly of a few naturally endowed individuals. If one or two simple rules are observed, the bowing can be executed with the utmost ease, but like all "fancy" bowings a sensitive control is necessary in order to ensure its successful accomplishment.

Staccato is but another instance of the hand and arm working in different planes. Perhaps I should here mention that for this reason no fancy bowings should be undertaken until legato bowings have been accomplished. I always take staccato last of all the bowings, as I find that otherwise it develops a cramped style and leads to the pupil moving the bow arm in a stiff and awkward manner. Further, as the bow is pressed slightly *into* the strings at the beginning of each note, pupils often develop a scratching tight tone. Properly played, staccato bowings are perhaps the most effective of all, but how rarely one hears them executed even passably well! All ordinary staccato bowings are played in the up bows, but remarkable effects are obtainable if they are also developed in the downward stroke.

Let us see how the up stroke can be developed, but firstly we will remember the following points:—

(1) That we begin as closely to the tip of the bow as possible.

(2) That only a small fraction of the bow is used for each stroke.

(3) That the bow remains in contact with the strings throughout.

(4) That an accent is given at the *beginning* of each note by means of the forefinger.

(5) That the bow rests quite stationary on the strings for the same length of time that it has taken to produce the previous note.

(6) That the attack given to each note is actually very slight, and that on no account should the bowing, as a result, become scratchy.

(7) Lastly, and by no means leastly, there should be no stiffness in the movement of the arm.

Now let us take our first stroke. To begin with we desire to move the bow over the strings for two inches from the point. In order to do this, we retain the tension of the first finger against the stick. *Take the stroke as rapidly as possible, at the same time releasing the pressure of the forefinger.* The first result will not be satisfactory. The forefinger will be released either not quickly enough or too soon, and the bow will move in a sluggish manner or skid. Let us repeat the performance, however, until successful. Then let us follow the first by another stroke in the same bow, and then a third, and so on, until the middle of the bow is reached. After this, we will begin once again and repeat the movements, this time using one inch of the bow. Between each stroke, the bow should rest on the strings without pressure for the same length of time occupied in playing the previous note. When this can be managed, we continue to use less and less bow until we can play a number of notes with a clean attack, using the minimum amount of bow. Do not attempt to play up staccato bowings beyond the middle (the balance) of the stick.

We will presume that so far we have progressed satisfactorily, and that now we desire to increase the speed. In this case it is important to remember that speed comes but gradually, so that it is useless endeavouring to run before we have learnt to walk. The more slowly speed is increased, the more surely will the effect be good. If we practise the bowing in the manner described for a considerable time we shall find that the constant pressure and relaxation of the forefinger leads to our acquiring a supple movement of the wrist, which enables us to play the notes with great rapidity. Then, however, we find that the bow is apt to run away with us. Let me explain why this happens—it is because we *begin* the bowing too rapidly, and it becomes impossible for the fingers to move at the same rate at the outset, and both, consequently, continue at different speeds. If, however, we begin staccato quite deliberately, slowly increasing the speed as we go along, we shall find that there is a very different result, and that both fingers and bow move in perfect unison.

I have taught staccato bowing to some hundreds of players, and so far, I have never experienced the slightest difficulty with the dullest pupil when the above rules have been observed.

Let me emphasise that an uncontrolled tremolo of the right hand is useless, and that in order to effect the bowing in the correct manner it is necessary to practise it for a considerable time quite slowly, very gradually increasing the speed as one progresses. On no account forget to turn the hand well in the direction of the bow throughout the stroke, as any stiffness in the fore-arm or upper-arm will only lead to scratchy and unsatisfactory results.

No finger flexion takes place in this or in *any* bowing executed at the point or the stroke will be ruined. The wrist merely rises as in ordinary legato bowing.

PART V.

CHAPTER XIX.

62. HOW TO PRACTISE DOUBLE STOPPING.

Intonation—Thirds.

In the study of double stopping, I find that thirds are at once the most difficult and useful of all exercises in double stopping. In addition to training the fingers they assist the ear more than any other interval. It would be well worth every violinist's time if he or she went through the whole book of Wilhelmj's Exercises in Thirds, which are so easily graduated that it is possible to begin them during the first term of one's study, and continue with them for the rest of one's life! I find that pupils without a very satisfactory sense of pitch have developed their hearing to quite an extraordinary extent by assiduously working at these studies. However good an ear any musician may possess, it needs developing before it can become perfect. We know that in the case of piano tuners men are employed irrespective of a knowledge of music, but they are gradually trained until their sense of pitch becomes perfect—or rather imperfect, for a piano has to be tuned out of tune in order that it may be played on with satisfactory results in every key. Therefore, let me give a few rules for the practice of exercises in thirds :—

(1) Sharps should be played really sharp, and flats really flat.

(2) In major thirds the third note will be played a full third, and in the minor a slightly fine third.

(3) Whole tones should be full; half tones, fine. By that I mean that whole notes are, if anything, fuller, and semitones, less.

(This also applies in the case of consecutive thirds.) It will be seen that "To him that hath shall be given, and from him that hath not shall be taken away even that which he seemeth to have." This is the principle of playing in tune. On the piano it is not possible to make one note sharp or another flat, but on the violin—as with the voice—we are enabled to play in just intonation. On the piano a sort of compromise has to be effected, as the same notes have to serve for sharps and flats; on the violin, no such expedient is necessary. If the simple rules I have given in the practice of double stopping are observed—particularly in thirds—the player's ear should benefit to a considerable extent.

All double notes should be practised in separate bows in the first instance, and only played slurred when they are quite in tune.

Having explained so much, it will be seen that the practice so often adopted of studying the violin with the pianoforte is discountenanced, and it will more likely lead to the marring than the development of a good ear.

63. SLIDING IN DOUBLE STOPPING.

When it is desired to slide from one position to another in double stopping, only the fingers which are actually used should be employed. The rules previously laid down in connection with sliding apply. The one explanation which it is necessary to make is when two notes are played on one set of strings, and the following two with the addition of an adjacent string. In this case it is obviously not possible to slide on *both* strings —therefore the slide should be made on the intermediate string common to both. It will be seen that the slides from one set of double notes to another which necessitate crossing over the strings (either in ascending or descending passages), are made on either the A or D string.

Thus it is only necessary to employ one finger for the slide and one string, not two. In slides to a higher position, the bow will leave the lower of the two strings during the slide and remain on the higher until the new position is reached, when it will be transferred to the strings required. With slides to a lower position the higher string is released during the slide by both bow and finger.

64. SIXTHS AND OCTAVES.

Sixths should be studied very carefully. Play them in the first position, using successively the first and second, the second and third, and the third and fourth fingers. They are excellent practice, as it is not easy to place the fingers on the strings in their new position in sufficient time on account of the fact that one at least of the fingers has been previously employed on another string; therefore the fingers themselves must be moved very quickly. At the outset they should be changed while the bow *rests* on the strings at the point or nut; then when this can be accomplished they must be moved at the change of the bow without arresting it. Later on, study them in the higher positions, using the same two fingers for each sixth. As a matter of fact, it is really more simple to play sixths in the higher positions—both in ascending and descending—than in the first.

The best method of practising octaves is to use them in the playing of scales. Great care should be observed to ensure that the second and third fingers do not rest on the strings. They should be lifted well out of the way, as when the higher positions are reached the first and fourth fingers come so closely together that they would be hampered by the presence of others between them.

The chief points to be observed in connection with double stopping are:—

(1) That the notes should be in tune!

(2) That the bow rests equally on both strings.

(3) That no finger not actually employed should be placed on the strings.

(4) That during sliding, only the fingers making the slide should remain on the fingerboard.

(5) That at first the lower note is accepted as being in tune and the higher corrected accordingly.

(6) That during sliding the fingers do not press too firmly on the strings.

It is useless to endeavour to alter first one finger and then the other—or both together! — as this leads to disastrous results. The first finger should be taken as the basis; be sure, therefore, that it slides the correct distance, and immediately make the fourth agree with it.

CHAPTER XX.

65. EXTENSIONS. TENTHS.

If a single instance were required to illustrate the hopelessly out-of-date methods usually employed in teaching the violin it would not be necessary for me to go further than the question of extensions.

The advice given is always the same, viz.: " To extend the fourth finger to the required note." This recommendation is made by teachers and in text books! Poor little fourth finger! How it must have been pulled out of joint during the last 250 years by thousands of aspiring violinists, and yet with all the pushing and shoving in the world hardly anybody's little finger can be made to extend beyond a semitone! What a waste of effort.

I have never seen or heard it explained that it is the first finger that enables us to play tenths and similar extensions, and not the fourth—or that extensions are made *backwards* by the aid of the first finger instead of forwards by the fourth as commonly supposed.

One moment's experiment will prove the truth of my statement. Take your violin and place the first finger on B (on the A string) in the first position—then, without allowing the hand to move, endeavour to extend the fourth finger to D (the tenth above). It will not take you many minutes to discover that you are attempting the impossible. Perhaps in a few cases when the hand is abnormally long C sharp may be reached, but most ordinary players will be unable to stretch beyond C natural. This is easily explained by the fact that the little finger is only slightly curved when placed on the strings in a comfortable position, and the most that can be accomplished by way of an

PLATE XIII.

POSITION OF FINGERS DURING RELAXATION.

(*See Chapter on Finger Action.*)

Photograph by Wykeham.]

PLATE XIII

extension is to straighten it, which will enable the finger to reach about a semitone above.

Now let us begin from the other end. Place the fourth finger on D with the hand in the third position and extend the first backwards (it may be necessary to place the side of the finger on the strings) at the same time straightening the fourth finger. It will be found that with a little practice the B on the A string is reached fairly easily by ordinary sized hands.

Therefore remember that all extensions can be accomplished by placing the hand in the position of the highest note and extending the first finger backwards, instead of allowing the hand to remain in the lowest position and endeavouring to stretch the weak little finger upwards.

CHAPTER XXI.

66. RIGHT-HAND PIZZICATO.

In the execution of this, the violinist should experience no difficulty, the strings being merely pulled or plucked by the forefinger of the right hand. The bow is held firmly in the hand so that the stick falls down the natural V between the thumb and the first finger, the nut of the bow being held in the hand.

The tip of the finger only should be used in pulling the strings, and the plucking should take place about three inches away from the bridge, so as not to come in contact with the resin on the strings.

In order to steady the hand, the tip of the right thumb is placed against the point of the finger-board to the right of the E string. Some players use their first and second fingers in playing pizzicato in rapid time, and there is no reason why this should not be done, as it possibly leads to greater facility. The quality of the tone produced may be varied according to the manner and position in which the strings are plucked, but on no account should the fingers hook underneath the strings, as this only leads to clumsy execution. With very little practice the player will find that he can manage right-hand pizzicato quite easily. The strings should not be pulled too forcibly but quite freely, as otherwise they will possibly jar against the end of the finger-board.

67. LEFT-HAND PIZZICATO.

In the performance of serious music this mode of pulling the strings is rarely, if ever, employed. Sometimes, in the case of emergency, a note—or possibly two—may be pulled by the fingers of the left hand, but in ordinary cases it is not necessary. The effect is chiefly used in the performance of music of the virtuoso type. Let us begin by practising it on the E string. Place the fourth finger firmly on B and pull it off the strings, at the same time pressing downwards; the E string will then be struck. Now let us do the same thing with the third finger, and then use the second and first in like manner. Having done this much, repeat the exercise, this time with the first finger pressed on the strings, so as to strike F. Then employ the second finger, when G results. Having accomplished this, let us place the whole of the four fingers on the strings, pulling them off one by one in succession, when each time we shall find that the note below is heard. It is important to remember that at the outset the fingers are pulled slightly downwards, as otherwise they will merely slip off the strings without sounding any note; but *directly* the note is struck the fingers are lifted in order to avoid adjacent strings.

When the notes on the E string can be played satisfactorily in the manner described, repeat the same exercises on the remaining strings, but in this case great care will have to be exercised in order to avoid pulling the open strings above.

It is hardly worth while endeavouring to perfect this form of pizzicato for its own sake, but it certainly should be practised in order to strengthen and obtain control over the fingers of the left hand. Needless to say, if one is anxious to astonish those who are desirous of being surprised, considerable facility can be obtained by assiduous practice, but it should be borne in mind that the violin is not an instrument to be "clowned" with. Paganini actually wrote shakes in left-hand pizzicato which have been subsequently performed by well-known virtuosi, but the effects were hardly particularly gratifying, and certainly not worth the labour involved in obtaining them.

68. HARMONICS.

Natural harmonics are partial tones of a higher pitch which accompany perfect musical sounds. Paganini introduced artificial harmonics, and thereby considerably enlarged the scope of the virtuoso's repertory. They are produced by changing the base of the harmonic by stopping the string with one finger and pressing another lightly against it at either a fifth, fourth or third.

Harmonic tones are particularly clear and beautiful, and if the finger is pressed sufficiently lightly against the note to be played, the result will be altogether gratifying. This, however, applies to natural harmonics. Artificial harmonics are by no means satisfactory, and are used chiefly in connection with virtuoso music.

Again, these are of considerable benefit if placed in the right category, and practised not so much for their immediate results as for the effect they have in developing left-hand control.

The first finger should be stopped firmly as for ordinary notes, and the third or fourth finger placed lightly but firmly (*i.e.*, without pressure but with control) on the strings. If too little pressure is employed the string will vibrate at the point of contact, and the harmonic will not speak readily, but it is far more likely that too much pressure will result in a husky note. It should be remembered that in harmonics the string vibrates on either side of the finger and not merely on the bow side. If the fingers are straightened more than in the playing of solid notes, harmonics can be played with greater ease, as the pad of the finger is more sensitive than the tip, and consequently the control becomes more perfect.

CHAPTER XXII.

69. THE SHAKE.

It is almost impossible to play even the shortest piece of music without encountering at least one shake. As we all know, shakes merely consist of very rapid and repeated alternations of one note with another. The chief point to be observed in the playing of shakes is that all the notes are equal and rhythmical, but without accent. Prolonged study is necessary before it is possible to play shakes in the manner described. To begin with we find that our fingers will not move quickly enough, and then when we endeavour to make them do so, the shake becomes unequal. Instead of having a series of notes of equal value as we should, we find that every note is of a different length. This at once gives rise to a feeling of laboriousness and fatigue, so that the result, instead of being one of light-hearted gaiety, is the very reverse.

The only method that I know which will produce a satisfactory shake is by learning, in the first instance, to raise and relax from the knuckles one finger at a time, and drop it on the strings in the shortest possible length of time. In order to do this, we must practise one shake at a time with each finger. It is rarely, indeed, that one has to play a shake of any length with the first finger, but at the same time it is necessary that we should be able to do it, as it leads to flexibility.

Let us begin with the second finger. Place the first finger on the strings, raise the second well above the strings, and having done so endeavour to strike as quickly as possible, leaving the finger on the strings for the minutest portion of a second, immediately returning it to the original position with the finger relaxed. Keep on repeating this many dozens of times. Do not endeavour to make the shakes equal, but after the finger has struck the strings allow it to remain above them for two or three seconds, during which time it should be relaxed; then repeat the operation. The chief point to be observed is that the finger, having touched the strings, leaves them immediately as though they were hot coals. Once again, it is the *lifting* that really matters, and controls the length of time that we remain on the strings far more than the actual dropping of the finger. Therefore, concentrate your mind entirely on the lifting, though I would impress upon you the fact that the finger must drop from its highest point to meet the strings with considerable velocity.

Having successfully accomplished one shake, proceed to play two, then three, and so on, always ensuring that they are of equal length. It follows that the quicker the shake, the less the finger can be lifted from the strings; so that if we are playing one shake it is possible for the finger to fall from a height; but if we are playing two, three, four or more in rapid succession, the finger can only be lifted a short way above the strings. However, in practising shakes endeavour to lift your fingers rather than raise them just above the note. In any case, be quite certain how many notes you are going to play in each shake, in order that you may get the necessary rhythmical effect.

It is useless endeavouring to develop a shake by means of a tremolo of the left hand. This, at the best, produces a bad shake which is anything but clear, and in addition, it leads to a lack of flexibility.

When a shake is placed over a dotted note, the former should continue during the length of the note minus the dot, the remainder of the note being held. Again, remember that if a shake is played before an accented note a turn must complete the shake, so that it is necessary to practise the turn by itself. This should be played in exactly the same time as the shake. There are numerous passages in which one has to hold a note and play a prolonged shake or number of shakes on others, so that it will be found an excellent plan when practising shakes to hold one or more of the remaining fingers on other strings either above or below the fingers in use.

The importance of the shake in the development of left-hand technique cannot be over emphasised; but it is essential that it should be made entirely from the fingers, without any stiffness or movement of the hand.

70. TREMOLO OR VIBRATO.

"A tremolo is in reality a slight alteration of the natural beats of a note, which serves to intensify it. A wave of sound is produced which seems to cause a more tense vibration of the note. The effect is produced by a slight alternate flattening and sharpening of each sound. In the case of organs and harmoniums, the tremolo (*vox humana*) is produced by tuning two sets of reeds to a slightly different pitch. On the violin, it is the result of flexibility of the hand and fingers which allows the hand to vibrate freely, causing the note to pulsate."

I have quoted the above in order that the reader may understand the exact nature of the effect that he is endeavouring to produce. Unfortunately, the tremolo or vibrato is only less abused than the slide. Once again, if used with taste the result is beautiful, but far more often than not it is merely employed in order to create the effect of a feverish sentiment. The pulsations of a good tremolo will be quite even and by no means too fast, but more often than not the player produces an exaggerated effect altogether lacking in dignity, and in anything but the best taste.

The tremolo is produced by rhythmical vibrations of the hand and fingers. It will therefore be seen that should any stiffness be apparent it will be impossible for these vibrations to take place. Let me again emphasise that the tremolo should be neither too fast nor too slow. In any case, avoid an exaggerated effect, as the note will then sound out of tune. Many violinists endeavour to produce the desired effect by means of pressing the finger tip very firmly against the string and by tightening the left wrist. It is altogether impossible to get satisfactory results in this way, as it is essential that the left wrist—and consequently the hand—should be quite free. If both work together in unison, the tremolo will be neither too fast nor too slow, but it is far more likely to be the former than the latter. The question is one of *using the natural balance of the finger when on the strings*, and when any stiffness or tightness is apparent in the muscles of the hand or fingers a satisfactory tremolo cannot be obtained. (See also Section XII.)

PART VI.

CHAPTER XXIII.

71. SIGHT READING AND MEMORISING.

Both sight reading and memorising are important factors in the development of a musician. In any language, as we become acquainted with it, we are able to understand the meaning of the words, and translate them at sight into modulated sentences without hesitation, and having repeated the same sentences several times, it is possible to say the passage without the aid of the book. Exactly the same results should be obtained in connection with music. In either case, we are employing a means of expression, and it is not more difficult to read and memorise in any one medium than another, provided, of course, that we are equally conversant with both. It follows, therefore, that before we make any attempts at sight reading, it is necessary for us to be thoroughly acquainted with the medium that we are using. For this reason, it is of little use giving sight-reading exercises on an instrument other than the voice to beginners. In fact, I may go so far as to say that it is a practice to be condemned.

Two processes are necessary in connection with sight reading. We have to understand the significance at sight of that which we observe, and then we must be able to translate it into sound. Unless we are thoroughly conversant with our medium and have the necessary technique to play the passage, we shall find some difficulty in the second part of the operation, for even though we understand that which we see, our lack of knowledge of the medium in which we are expressing ourselves makes it difficult for us to speak quickly. Now sight reading necessitates above all else that we can translate thought into sound at a moment's notice. To do this, we must at all times have a technique superior to the demands of the music, for otherwise we shall hesitate over particular passages.

Sight reading may be developed quite easily as technique progresses, but the music chosen should never be too difficult, and in any case the pupil should be able to play it quite easily, so that the actual technique presents no difficulties. With beginners, sight reading is apt to do more harm than good unless undertaken under the supervision of the teacher, as the pupil will make numberless mistakes without being aware of them. Instead, therefore, of gaining facility in sight reading, there will merely be a slovenliness in performance. When the pupil has progressed sufficiently he should be able to gain experience by practising sonatas, trios and quartets with other musicians, when it will be necessary for him to keep his place, but it is obviously absurd for him to attempt this when, even though he may not lose his place, he is unable to play half the passages with which he comes in contact.

It is necessary to think and feel the significance of the notes we see before we can express their meaning.

Memorising is as important as sight reading, as it is of little use if we are able to read something and immediately afterwards forget that which we have read. In any case, it is a habit quite easy to acquire, and merely a matter of practice. We know quite well that if we keep repeating a certain sentence, after a short time we are able to say it from memory; and exactly the same thing applies to music. All that is necessary is that we should take passages that are not too long, and then gradually add other passages as we become acquainted with the first. In this way, we are able in a short time to memorise at great ease. It is better to take complete phrases, as then a knowledge of the structure of the music is obtained, so that our efforts are beneficial in two directions.

It is always preferable, if possible, to play solos from memory, as it means we must have practised the music quite thoroughly.

In addition, our playing gains in confidence when we do not have to employ any of our attention by looking at the notes, as would otherwise be the case. Besides, in the performance of any work it is necessary to think well ahead, as one does when reading a book, in order to gain the sense. This is not possible to the same extent when one is occupied in reading notes.

There is little doubt that music which is memorised is rarely, if ever, forgotten, and with only slight practice the complete work may be played again, even though it has been discarded for a considerable period.

CHAPTER XXIV.

72. CONTROLLED MOVEMENT AND CONCENTRATION.

VIOLINISTS must realise that every movement they make whilst playing should be the direct result of complete mental and physical control.

We know quite well that when we relax we become lazy, and that whilst we are making an effort to concentrate on something the action keeps us awake. If we relax our muscles whilst playing the violin, there is a consequent mental relaxation and loss of control. Control creates a tense condition of the body and mind—or rather the latter is an essential of control. How often have we heard the expression that when a person is "worked up" he can accomplish almost anything? This merely means that when we are "worked up" our minds and bodies are in a tense condition, which enables us to concentrate on the work in hand. If one is tense, one can concentrate; but when relaxation takes place, concentration disappears. Whilst we are playing, it is necessary to sustain concentration to the utmost of our power, and it is only when we have completed our performance that we may relax either mentally or physically. It is this tense concentration which places such a great strain on an artist. He may not relax for one second from the moment he begins to play until he has finished.

We all know quite well how the slightest noise will lead to an artist's "breaking down." This just means that for the moment his attention has been attracted by something other than the work in hand, and as a result his mind has relaxed from that which he was endeavouring to execute.

We should try to develop concentration by every means in our power, and endeavour to get *into* our music to the oblivion of all else.

The performance of even a slight piece of music is only made possible as the result of sustained concentration. The most extraordinary alertness is essential. Therefore, it is not possible to convey sustained thought through a physical medium unless mind and muscles are in a relatively tense condition. In order to give an inner life and spirituality to that which we would express, we must be alive ourselves, really alive, both mentally and physically.

73. ON RELAXATION.

Nervousness and Stiffness.

The secret of left-hand technique is relaxation, and unless the muscles of each finger are released following their employment, left-hand technique can never be obtained.

Stiffness is mental—the result is physical, but the cause mental. Stiffness ruins all artistic achievement, and makes technical facility impossible. In addition, it is the chief contributing factor in nervousness. The latter again is mental, but nervousness causes us to tighten up our muscles, and by this action we render ourselves more nervous.

There is a constant reaction between the two—the nerves and the muscles. Each contributes to the state of the other. Therefore, we must endeavour at all times to combat stiffness, and it will be found that in so doing we are combating nervousness. I cannot impress this point on players too strongly, for I have never found stiffness without its coadjutor nervousness.

Now let us look into the matter a little further. Stiffness is the result of discomfort. Herein lies the secret of the whole situation. Discomfort affects us both mentally and physically. We cannot be at ease unless we are comfortable.

This is something to begin with. We have to be comfortable in order to avoid stiffness and consequent nervousness. Unless we are comfortable we cannot gain technical facility, so that the *manner* in which we do everything is of the utmost importance.

In certain positions it is not possible to be comfortable, and unless the violin and the bow are held in a manner calculated to give the utmost control with the least effort we find that our muscles stiffen and render our movements awkward. This has a mental effect, and either makes us nervous when we are not naturally so, or is a contributing factor to existing nervousness.

The antidote to both stiffness and nervousness is relaxation, and in order to relax we must have complete mental and physical control.

The fingers should be relaxed (rested) after each movement. The more they are worked the more must they be rested, otherwise it is equivalent to asking a human being to work throughout the day and night without break. Let us consider what the result would be.

Fatigue would ensue, and after a short

time that work which, when fresh, was easily within his scope, would become difficult when weary. The methods found satisfactory if employed naturally would become ineffective when used unnaturally. Muscles other than those ordinarily used would be brought into play to bolster up the fatigued and failing ones, and as they were not suited to their job, they would lead to stiffness and consequent nervousness.

Exactly the same remarks apply when we endeavour to acquire technique, and the same results accrue if we employ wrong muscles or those which we are using become tired.

Nervousness and stiffness are boon companions.

In left-hand technique only those muscles which regulate the movement of the fingers should be used, and where the muscles of the hand and thumb are stiffened technical facility is retarded. The same principle applies to bow technique.

CHAPTER XXV.

74. HOW TO BECOME A MUSICIAN.

In the previous chapters I have dealt on a broad basis with practically the whole of violin technique. I have endeavoured to show, in so far as it is possible to do in a book, how violin technique may be acquired. However, this is but the beginning of things, and I have made no mention of that which is far more important, viz., how one becomes a musician. As I stated in the opening chapters, there are three essentials necessary to ensure the success of the individual who decides to take up the study of any instrument, or who wishes to become an artist—professional or amateur. He must be able :—

(1) To understand.
(2) To feel.
(3) To express.

I have merely given the reader an idea of the technique used in expression, but beyond this he has first to understand, then to feel, and still to express. What have we, then, to develop in order that we may now have something to say? Surely there is only one answer, and that is—ourselves.

In order to illustrate my point a little further, I should like to tell the following short story:—

A violinist once came to me and told me that while he could play the notes without difficulty, he always felt that he really hadn't anything worth saying, and asked my advice as to the best means of becoming a musician. After we had chatted for a short time I learned that he had been the pet of the family all his life. He had never known hardship or suffering of any kind, and had always lain on a bed of cotton wool. In addition, he had not gone in for sports. His parents, in order to save him from coming in contact with the world, did not send him to a public school. He had had a private tutor, and every moment between had been occupied in practising the violin. He was quite young, as far as I remember, and had not come of age. Indeed, he was what the world would call, "a very nice clean boy," but I do not think that I ever felt more sorry for anybody in my life; he was altogether undeveloped mentally and physically. My answer to his query as to how he should become a musician surprised, and, I am afraid, rather hurt him. I told him to dispense with the assistance of his relations and go out into the world and earn his own living. He said that he could not unless he played in an orchestra, and his people would not like him to do that. I explained that it was no use trying to become a musician by going on with his studies on the violin, or by playing in an orchestra, as he really was not developed enough to do any good with either. What I meant was, he should walk out into the world with nothing in his pocket, and then he might learn that which otherwise he could never understand. If from this start he could make good, he would probably one day stand a chance of becoming a *musician;* but that if he took a broader and more easily traversed road, he would probably never arrive anywhere.

I regret to say that this unfortunately placed young man never made good, and it is hardly necessary to say that everything was against his doing so. My advice had come too late, and had I been older I should have known that it would be better to keep my thoughts to myself, as they were inappropriate to the situation. I only tell this story in order to illustrate that he was without understanding, therefore had nothing to express. His deeper emotions were untouched, and his feeling for music was shallow and sentimental. Possibly, and all too probably, he might not have made good in any case—the start was a very bad one—but the suggested remedy—though drastic—would perhaps have left him better able to fight the battle of life than he eventually became. In my ignorance I did not realise that it would have taken a super-man to carry out my well-intentioned but in the circumstances very silly advice. Needless to say, such advice was *not* carried out.

It is just fifteen years ago since I gave that advice, and only a short time since that man came to see me. He was literally in rags. His relations had lost their money during the war; he had long ago sold his violin, and had been endeavouring to pick up a livelihood as best he might. Unfortunately his suffering had come too late to be of any avail. His early life had been too easy for him to benefit by such experience at the age of nearly forty.

Perhaps this sad story will illustrate my meaning. It is necessary for the artist to have lived a real life, and not an artificial one, before he can be expected to make good. Without difficulties of one kind or another—I do not mean starvation or any one hardship in particular—the depths of our feelings remain untouched, and consequently we know nothing of the meaning of life. We have nothing to express; nothing really worth saying, and if we said anything it would be stated with so little conviction as to carry no weight. I am sorry for the man who is born rich, should that man desire to become an artist. What a wonder Mendelssohn was to have done so much! Some people say so little, but consider his chances.

Practically every great musician had one struggle on top of another throughout his life, but the fighting and conquering of difficulties led to ultimate success. The cotton wool musician is the merest travesty of an artist; therefore, would you be a musician, work hard and live hard.

A knowledge of a medium of expression does not make one an artist, but this, combined with a knowledge and understanding of the deeper emotions of life will help you to become one. Therefore, develop your brains, body and understanding. Cultivate a knowledge of the other arts, for this knowledge will help you to become a musician.

CHAPTER XXVI.

75. MUSICAL DEVELOPMENT.

THE musical development of the pupil will be helped very considerably in the first instance in the choice of a suitable master. He will start the pupil in the right path, and show him the way he should go. Then, if the pupil is sufficiently developed, the rest should not be difficult.

"The selection of suitable music is a matter that should occupy the serious consideration of every pupil and player. In the case of a young pupil, not only the character, but, in all probability, the whole musical life is influenced by a judicious or injudicious choice. The germ fostered by the teacher grows with the growth of the pupil; the mind is influenced thereby, and the musical faculty is developed on lines laid down during the most impressionable period of life. It is therefore hardly necessary to say how important it is that only music calculated to educate and develop the mind on rational musical lines should be selected."

In order to gain a more intimate knowledge and understanding of the works of the great masters, in addition to studying them, read their lives. This should help you to obtain the atmosphere so necessary to real understanding. Begin where music began, studying the seventeenth and eighteenth century composers whose works present few technical difficulties, and then proceed to develop along with the development of music. On no account begin by studying modern, or ultra modern music, as you will not be in a position to appreciate its intrinsic value. Remember at all times that it is the musician's *mind* that matters, and in order to develop this on rational lines it is necessary to begin at the beginning. When the early classics have been studied, it is sufficient time to study modern music. In any case, avoid sentimental music of the drawing-room type; it is pernicious and utterly demoralising. Music does not only appeal to the emotions; it has a primary appeal to the intellect—or rather, it should have. When it does not make an intellectual appeal, one is forced to the conclusion that opportunity has been lacking, or that the higher qualities of the mind are in abeyance.

"The highest artistic expression is not purely emotional any more than it is entirely intellectual. I consider that it is a combination of both these qualities, with the brain always predominating. I should therefore prefer to describe the ideal musical expression as being intellectually controlled emotion."

Besides a knowledge of all the violin works of the great masters, it is necessary for the pupil to be acquainted with all important pianoforte, chamber, orchestral and choral music of every period. These works can easily be studied by means of miniature scores. In order that any executive artist may be able to interpret the works of masters, it is necessary that he should gain an insight into the workings of their minds. This can only be obtained through a thorough knowledge of their music.

CHAPTER XXVII.

76. CONCLUSION.

Dont's.

In conclusion I should like to state that it has not been my intention to provide a complete violin tutor in these altogether inadequate chapters. If, however, they help the violinist in even the choice of a master and inform him that which he should expect to be taught, I feel that they will not altogether have failed in their purport. No amount of reading books on violin playing will turn out a violinist—much less a musician; but there are times when such a work is useful for reference, and in such I trust that these few chapters will help the reader over some difficulties. There are many points I have not touched upon; I have merely endeavoured to lay down broad principles upon which violin technique is founded. Had I gone beyond this, I should in all probability have wandered out of my depth, and led the pupil out of his.

There are, however, still one or two things that I should like to mention, and perhaps if I put them in the form of "Don'ts" it would be the quickest way for me to state them.

1. Don't pose.

2. Don't acquire mannerisms.

3. Don't try to impress anybody but yourself.

4. Don't look or be awkward.

5. Don't endeavour to "clown" with your violin; you can "clown" without it.

6. Don't exercise your fingers without your mind.

7. Don't attempt to begin at the top.

8. Don't be content to stay at the bottom.

9. Don't be flattered by praise of the uninitiated.

10. Don't try to astonish.

11. Don't try to please.

12. Don't mistake technique for art.

13. Don't aim at art for art's sake, but rather art for life's sake.

14. Don't despise that which you don't understand.

15. Don't worship that which you understand, unless you are certain that you have understanding.

16. Don't lose your own individuality and take on another's.

17. Don't attempt to express yourself unless you feel that you have something to say.

18. Don't be insincere.

19. Don't play down to your audience, as if you are an artist you can never play above it.

20. Don't worship tradition, but don't break away from it until you are conversant with it.

21. Don't let your judgment be blinded by Mr. Voluptuousness's tone; Mr. Blacksmith's power; Mr. Lack-Control's abandon;

Mr. Weak-Knee's delicacy; Mr. Heat's warmth; and Mr. Make-Belief's show-off.

22. Don't *seek* success, it will find you.

23. Don't make too much of your virtues or too little of your faults.

24. Don't be disheartened if you don't succeed, and don't give up—just don't, but go on struggling until you "DO."

THE END.

CPSIA information can be obtained at www.ICGtesting.com
Printed in the USA
BVOW05*0535130415

395770BV00003B/7/P